The l

Also by Judith Pinhey
and available as a
Fount Paperback

The Music of Love

The Dance of Life

Judith Pinhey

Edited by Teresa de Bertodano

With a Foreword by
Robert Llewelyn

Fount
An Imprint of HarperCollinsPublishers

Fount Paperbacks is an Imprint of
HarperCollins*Religious*
Part of Harper Collins*Publishers*
77–85 Fulham Palace Road, London W6 8JB

First published in Great Britain
in 1992 by Fount Paperbacks

1 3 5 7 9 10 8 6 4 2

A catalogue record for this book is
available from the British Library

ISBN 0 00 627598-2

Typeset by Medcalf Type Ltd, Bicester, Oxon

Printed and bound in Great Britain by
HarperCollinsManufacturing Glasgow

To my brothers and sisters
at St James's Church who have
given me so much.

Contents

ix

Foreword

Here is a book which, like its predecessor *The Music of Love*, will make personal appeal to many who buy it. But I believe it will appeal too to others, unlikely to buy or even read religious books, who may stumble across it as a gift in the post, a loan from their pastor before going into hospital, a casual browse by a prisoner through the chapel bookshelf. For this reason it may be that many who have pastoral cures will be glad to own copies which they can lend (and be prepared to lose) to people open to receive support in some critical period of their lives.

Every reader of *The Music of Love* will want to rejoice with Judith Pinhey and to thank God with her for the healing of Nicholas, her son. She tells the full story in the introduction which follows. Many readers will have held Nicholas before God in their prayers, and Judith and Jonathan are truly grateful. One of the beauties of such a book as *The Dance of Life* and its forerunner is that the readership is drawn together in a communion of support and love.

Robert Llewelyn

Acknowledgements

I should like to express my warmest thanks to Robert Llewelyn for his advice and encouragement. I am grateful to my family and others who read and commented on the typescripts of my introduction, and especially to Teresa de Bertodano for her help in choosing the passages.

Introduction

The passages in this book have been chosen from about two hundred which I wrote between July 1989 and August 1991. I do not hear the words with my ears and I do not set out to compose them. They are formed in my heart in silent prayer, and I believe I receive them, as far as I am enabled, from Jesus. This may happen at any time and in any place when I am quiet and listening attentively. The love of the crucified and risen Lord Jesus Christ is always the central truth and the deepest reality out of which the words come.

Many people long to know God intimately and to experience his love. When people tell me that these words help them to know the presence of Jesus and to hear him speaking directly to them, I am filled with wonder at the power of the Holy Spirit to glorify Jesus and to make him real to us. He accepts each of us by his grace and gives us exactly the right gifts to use in his service for the good of all, so that giving and receiving may flourish in our common life and flow out. I believe that these words are God's way of using the natural gifts he has given me.

Some of the passages are written as prayers, but the form in which most of them are written – in the first person, as from Jesus – raises questions for some people about authority. I place myself under the authority of the Bible and the Church, recognizing that there are different interpretations of the Bible, and that "the Church" means different things to different people. I am a Christian first and then an Anglican, but I also owe a great deal to other

Christian traditions. Intuitive insights can be misleading because they are subjective, and they must be rigorously tested. If they are truly given by the Holy Spirit they can bring light and life and health.

In *The Music of Love* I have tried to explain more fully how I receive these words and I have also written briefly about our son's illness. Nicholas suffered from Post Viral Fatigue Syndrome from the age of twenty-one, and continued to get worse for seven and a half years until November 1990. Then he began to make a remarkable recovery. He has missed practically the whole of his twenties, when a young man goes out and makes his own way in the world. Now, once again, he is able to live an active and independent life. I delight to believe that God's healing grace came through the prayers of many people and the skill of the medical profession, and I ask you to rejoice with us and give thanks to God.

There is still much controversy about Post Viral Fatigue Syndrome, which is thought to affect about 70,000 people in Britain. Nicholas was told by one doctor: "There's no cure for this illness. You'll have to accept that there's nothing we can do." Another said: "You must be mad. Why aren't you at work?" Such contradictory advice is not unusual and adds to the misery of sufferers and their families.

I have found that many doctors do not like the name "Myalgic Encephalomyelitis" (ME), because it denotes a disease process. Most prefer to use "Chronic Fatigue Syndrome" (CFS) in general, or "Post Viral Fatigue Syndrome" (PVFS) when there is laboratory evidence (as in Nicholas's case) of infection at onset.

Most people recover from PVFS within a few years but some do not. By the summer of 1989 Nicholas had been living with us for eighteen months so that he could be cared for, and his symptoms were very severe. We were extremely concerned about his immobility and isolation. He seemed to be in a downward spiral of desolation and despair.

People with PVFS need realistic hope, and this is what Nicholas was given by Dr Simon Wessely, a psychiatrist who has worked with PVFS patients at the National Hospital for Nervous Diseases. Misconceptions about PVFS abound and I shared many of these until I saw Nicholas's recovery with my own eyes. What happened will not make much sense without some medical details, so in the next few paragraphs I am quoting and paraphrasing from Dr Wessely's article "Depression and the Post Viral Fatigue Syndrome" (available from the ME Association), but any mistakes are my own.

Dr Wessely regards PVFS as "a genuine and serious illness" which "affects both mind and body in equal measure". His approach is based on the view that some viral infections can cause biochemical changes in the part of the brain which controls mood, energy, sleep and appetite, and that these changes are clinically indistinguishable from those found in major depression. For a long time I thought Nicholas's depression was a reaction to his illness. As I now understand it, it *was* his illness.

In PVFS, people often suffer from an atypical depression. They become more emotional, irritable and agitated. As in any depression, there may be severely disabling physical and mental fatigue, impairment of memory, headaches, muscle pain, tingling, gastro-intestinal problems, dizziness, tinnitus, chest pain and sensations of altered temperature. Light and sound may cause almost intolerable distress. Symptoms of anxiety are common: panic attacks, hyperventilation, palpitations, tremor and feelings of tension, fear and dread.

Fear of symptoms that are unpredictable and uncontrollable, as in PVFS, is particularly likely to lead to phobias, and these are common in severely affected patients. Nicholas could not open his eyes or allow any light or fresh air into his room. He ate an increasingly limited diet and refused to take anti-depressants.

Dr Wessely has developed a pragmatic approach to treatment and management using anti-depressants and cognitive behavioural therapy. He says: "A surgeon doesn't need to know the make of the car that ran over you to treat your broken leg." He starts with the symptoms as they are here and now, no matter what the cause. This is very good news for people with PVFS, although under that umbrella there may be more than one kind of condition, and I do not know what might help in any particular case.

My husband Jonathan and I were pleased and relieved, when, in December 1989, Nicholas decided to start a cognitive behavioural therapy programme under a local psychiatrist who had gained his confidence and continued to build up a relationship of trust with him. He had suggested this approach and generously gave an enormous amount of time in home visits and telephone calls to support Nicholas and us in the undertaking.

Behaviour therapy is not an exercise programme. It aims to help the patient to do, in a safe and controlled way, the activities that he or she has been avoiding. Cognitive therapy aims to help the patient to use conscious thoughts in a way which changes attitudes and promotes recovery. Most patients take anti-depressants as part of the programme, but Nicholas hoped that he could improve without taking drugs.

He started by sitting in a chair for five minutes each day and it did him no harm. Within a few months he was able, several times a day, to walk twenty lengths of his bedroom, sit in a chair for half an hour and walk to the lavatory, but he could not tackle the phobias, and from June 1990 he became steadily worse.

I believe that from January 1986 onwards I received many passages promising Nicholas's healing. On 7 June 1990, as part of a longer passage, I received these words: "I will heal Nicholas before the snow melts in the spring." I questioned this in my mind and the words continued: "I mean the coming spring." My first thought was: "We haven't even had any snow for four years." When the words are predictive, which is not often, the questions begin: "Is this God's will or is it wishful thinking? Is it reality or is it the avoidance of reality?" I had to live in this uncertainty, watching, listening, awaiting events which alone could confirm or deny the words, but I think they helped to keep alive in me a firm hope, against all appearances, that Nicholas would live and be well.

I put my faith in God once again, trusting him whatever his will might be. I prayed: "Lord, heal Nicholas, but if not, let him die outright. Don't let him carry on like this." This was my honest desire and I saw no reason to pretend otherwise.

I began to feel desperate as time went on, and in August I prayed: "Lord, give me a sign that all this really is in your hands. I know we're not supposed to ask for signs, but here I am and I'm asking for one." The next day our elder daughter telephoned to say that she and our son-in-law were expecting their first child, our first grandchild. Some may say that this was a coincidence. To me it was a gracious sign of hope, a reassurance that the creative power of love and the gift of life come from God. I received it as the sign I had asked for and it was a great comfort and strength to me. How we all rejoiced when, seven months later, Nicholas was the first member of the family to visit his little nephew in hospital!

By October Nicholas had not opened his eyes for two and a half years and we were particularly concerned that he had not spoken for several months. I could not forget the words about healing "in the spring", but he seemed terribly ill and we did not know why.

I had often wondered: "How could God get through to someone in this condition?" But God moves in his own way and in his own time. Suddenly, on the morning of 22 November 1990, Nicholas said: "He's done it . . . God. I think it'll be all right." He told us later that he had been enabled to give in to God and to trust him. This experience was a letting go on every level. He went into a depressive stupor and was taken into hospital. He had reached rock bottom and found that God was there.

We were clearly told that Nicholas might die and we were ready to welcome that outcome. Because he was *in extremis* he was given a course of Electroconvulsive Therapy (ECT) and this was dramatically effective. He came out of the stupor after two weeks and immediately began to open his eyes and talk.

Dr Wessely explained to us later that it is thought that ECT works by causing very rapid and persistent changes in the levels of certain chemicals in the brain which are implicated in the cause of severe depression. It became clear to us then that Nicholas could not have recovered until his very severe depression had been dealt with. Dr Wessely also said: "For the record I am not aware of any other incidents in which ECT has been used in definable ME/CFS."

Soon Nicholas was transferred to a psychiatric ward for rehabilitation. The experience of trust was the healing of the phobias and they fell away within a few weeks. He was able to eat normally, go for walks, cycle, read, watch television, enjoy the company of his friends, buy a second-hand car and make plans for the future. Prolonged inactivity and a limited diet had made him very weak and thin, but gradually his muscles became stronger and he gained weight.

Nicholas had arranged to drive from Cambridge to Leeds to stay with his younger sister and brother-in-law as soon as he was discharged from hospital on 8 February 1991. Two days before that, on 6 February, there was a heavy fall of snow and he had to wait until 11 February for the roads to clear sufficiently. Healing is always a process that continues on various levels, but 8 February is a significant date and the snow was far from melting on that day.

I have pondered this fall of snow which was so clearly mentioned in the words of 7 June 1990. The snow speaks to me of transfiguration. It is an image of God's down-to-earth beauty and goodness. He covers the earth with the pure, dazzling brightness of his glory, bringing radiance and joy. But the snow is not only an image. It actually fell – a large quantity of it over a wide area. It was a totally external factor over which neither I nor anyone else had any control. Another coincidence? I do not know, but I usually like to have things both ways, so, without claiming any special intervention, and without encroaching upon a mystery, I call it an act of God.

Some people have called Nicholas's recovery "a miracle" and, truly, it was a wonderful happening. There are conflicting views as to what kind of evidence is needed to substantiate claims of healing, and some dubious claims are made. Healing is a gift of God's love and we receive it, as we receive all his gifts, by faith. It is impossible to prove or disprove anything. I believe that in this case God was working, as he so often does, not against or apart from the psychological and physical laws, but with them and through them.

I take great pleasure in the interweaving of the medical and spiritual aspects of this story. I see it as a clear demonstration that the different parts of our lives are all one. The passages in this book proclaim the same truth: every kind of reality is God's reality and he has made everything holy.

I am sometimes asked how I coped with Nicholas's illness. God was my rock and standing on that rock was like standing on the edge of a precipice. I had to learn that there is one sound tree that I can hold on to if I let go of everything else. I felt that Jesus was with me all the time, illuminating the darkness with the light of his love. Indeed, without this, I am sure I could not have continued to receive his words. The pain was no less and sometimes I felt anxious, but Jesus is always the same. Whatever my circumstances may be, he is my hope and his presence is my joy.

Jonathan and I shared the sadness and difficulties of the situation and supported each other. We have different strengths and weaknesses and together we did what neither of us could have done alone.

We received constant love, support and practical help in caring for Nicholas from our family and many other people. Friends continued to ask how he was, fearing to hear, but asking none the less, because they knew how much their sympathy meant to us. A neighbour who sat with him for a few minutes every week said: "He is my friend."

Thousands of people, known and unknown, prayed for Nicholas, for Jonathan and me, and for our family, and we are deeply grateful. Prayer is not a last resort but the best gift someone can give. To be prayed for at the same time humbles me and lifts me up. To be held in someone else's heart before God makes available to me God's power to unite all things in himself. I cannot say how prayer works – it certainly does not change God's mind, although it may change me – but our interdependence in prayer is a source of great joy to me.

As Nicholas's illness seemed to close in on him he felt angry and embittered. After his recovery he said: "I was in hell." To be in hell is to be separated from God but on the cross Jesus took that separation into himself. His faithful love is stronger than our anger and hatred, and now nothing can separate us from him. He has become one with the whole human race and holds all created things in his pierced hands.

I have never felt abandoned by God and I pray especially for those who suffer in this way. I see our life as flowing from the cross through the eucharist, where together we give thanks for the life-giving death of Jesus. We all belong to each other, within the Church and beyond, because we all belong to God. The Church, the community of grace, is called to consider no one an outcast, but to be the servant of all, a sign of God's suffering love and a sign, therefore, of his joy.

This faith was deepened by the experience of caring for Nicholas. Going into his dark, enclosed room was like going into a black hole. My natural way is to knock twice, but on Nicholas's door I used to knock three times: "In the name of the Father and of the Son and of the Holy Spirit." Then I would go in and see a terribly sick, physically depleted young man, lying in great pain with his eyes closed, mentally and emotionally in torment, diminished, humanly speaking, almost to nothing. Medically, I was living in a fog, but I knew with exceptional clarity that even my very imperfect human love did not depend on a response. There were no strings attached. Whatever Nicholas did or did not do, wanted or did not want, deserved or did not deserve, I loved him because the reality of his being was given by God and exists most truly in God.

How much more God loves us, diminished as we are by our human limitations. He believes in us. He changes "I am not" into "I am". If we are hard on ourselves we shall be hard on others. As we learn to have compassion on ourselves, we shall be given a compassionate heart for all the world. God loves all people with a perfect and immeasurable love, not because we are good, but because he is good. We are preoccupied with credits and debits when all the time his love is free.

The events I have described are unimportant except for those who were affected by them, but because I participated in them to a small extent, God is forming me through them and helping me to know him. Countless people throughout the ages have drawn meaning out of their suffering and found renewal. For me, the meaning of suffering and newness of life are in the cross. I have no right to expect freedom from suffering and my egotism is confronted and challenged by the One whose power is shown in weakness and self-giving. If I allow myself to be torn apart I am made whole. If I can recognize the depths of my feelings and accept the anguish, I find myself in a spacious place.

This has led me to reflect on the meaning of freedom.

God has given us free will, but how free are we when we are bound by fear? We are free when we choose life, relationship, goodness, justice, peace, celebration – God himself. We are free when, like Jesus, we choose what God has chosen for us. When we choose less we are our own worst enemy, and the chronic sickness of one generation is passed on to the next. God knows that our deepest need is to be freed from fear, to trust him, and to know his unfailing love in the midst of danger, evil, destruction and finally death. Gently he says: "Don't be afraid," and patiently he encourages us to take him at his word.

I am sometimes asked if I have any regrets. My answer is: "You can't say what might have been. What is *is*." I have some sad memories, but which of us has not? I am learning how irrelevant it is to impute blame. From God's point of view we are all on a level. Only One is lifted up and he is lifted up on a cross. In his mercy nothing is wasted and nothing is lost. He is able to take our fragility and make us fit for eternal life. I trust him to bring good out of everything.

Someone may think: "What about me? My suffering continues." What can I say? When I look at the cross, always contemporary, and begin to glimpse the glory that is revealed, I can say: "While anyone suffers, Jesus suffers, and the point of it is love. There isn't any other point."

The first words I ever received came to me on 26 November 1985: "I will pour out my Spirit upon you in love and healing. You will see the wonders of my kingdom and you will praise my holy name." At that time I could not imagine what these words might mean. They seemed too good to be true. It was like being plunged into deep water – refreshing and exhilarating – but it took my breath away. Now I know that these words speak of the kingdom which is here and now, if we have eyes to see it, because it is given by the God who is more down to earth than we are.

The dance of life is the new life in which God holds us

and refreshes us. We are often out of step and we do not want to go where he is leading, but this dance is his grace in us. We dance alone with him as we look inward, and in company with his whole creation as he turns us to look outward. The music of God's love is the silent music of our hearts, and when we hear it in stillness we are part of the dance of his life.

God reveals himself through symbols and images, the language that our hearts can understand and respond to, but we need to remember that all images are relative and provisional. They point to a reality beyond themselves. We cannot speak without them, but when we use them we are saying "as if". God is neither father nor mother, neither wind nor fire, neither music nor dancing. I am continually struck by the fact that the passages in this book are completely inadequate to express God who is the mystery beyond all words and images, so I offer them, relying on the Spirit of Jesus to make them live.

Our turning to God is painfully slow and takes not less than a lifetime. God always takes the initiative. He opens deaf ears and blind eyes and gives us the gift of faith. He draws us into a relationship with him. He gives us the confidence to know ourselves a little more clearly and to begin an exploration of love. He is utterly enmeshed and embroiled in the raw material of our everyday lives. He is always where we are now, and one way or another he will surprise us with his nearness. Our part is to listen to the Word of life, to be simple and direct, to ask for his help and to look to him expectantly.

JUDITH PINHEY
August 1991

I kiss your footprints in the dust

Do you think I was remote from heaven when I came down to earth – remote as I gave the word and touch of healing, remote as I ate and drank with sinners? No, I was not remote.

How can you tell the Saviour's love for the nature he took?

My love for my mother is love for the one who chose to obey and gave birth to the Son of God. My love for the stable is love for all who are poor. My love for the workshop is love for the material things of earth, transformed by human hands. My love for my Father's house consumes me always and everywhere. My love for the hills of Galilee is the shepherd's love for his sheep. My love for the lake, as I rested in the lap of the storm, is love for all who are hard pressed and almost overcome, assailed by many a danger and troubled by many a woe.

All this love, love beyond telling, is the reality of my love for the reality of your life. This holy love stoops to kiss your footprints in the dust of the earth. It kneels before you and washes your feet.

You are not remote from me. I have made myself of the earth and I will never be removed.

The word of life

The word of life is given by my Spirit. It enters the mind and sinks into the heart. There the heart that knows me has made ready a bed for cultivation and the seed begins to grow.

In this operation all the grace is mine – grace in nourishing, grace in growing, grace in bearing fruit.

Like a seed in the earth my word is hidden in your heart, like a child growing in the womb, like a new creation rising from the tomb.

When you receive my word, things long hidden in darkness come to light and my being expands and enlarges your heart.

You are pregnant with me and you will bring forth my love and my truth. These, in turn, are manifested as the word of life, bearing fruit a hundredfold for my kingdom.

Look at the fig tree

Look at the fig tree. Its leaves are broad and lobed like the five fingers of a hand. Its fruit is soft and pear-shaped, containing many seeds.

You cover yourself with fig-leaves, thinking that you can hide yourself from me. Fig-leaves will no more cover you than your two hands with fingers outstretched. You must learn to stand naked before me. Until you stand before me in honest openness, revealing to yourself and to me what you are, we can have no conversation, you and I.

You are like a fig picked up out of the dust, small and hard. That fig was deprived of the life-giving sap and has fallen off before its prime. It is of no use, of no significance at all. It will never ripen and its seeds will never grow. No one will notice the fruit that came to nothing. No one will even consider what might have been.

I can do the impossible. I will pick up the withered fruit of the fig tree and reattach it to the branch. There it will grow plump and healthy. It will ripen and its flesh will be delicious to the taste.

A fig on the branch hangs like a bag full of treasure. If you are alive with my life, I am your treasure and you are full of me.

Light in your darkness

Light in the eyes but never too bright to look at, light in the mind but never too full to see, light in the heart, the light of my love that seeks you – this light is the majesty of my power over the darkness of death, the light which is the life of the world.

When you are in utter darkness, when sorrow plunges you into despair, when hope is an empty cavity and tomorrow a nothingness that will not go away, this light is a pinprick in the depth of dread. All the light that streams from my risen glory is refracted by the lens of the cross on to that nadir of need.

This light, the light of heaven's praise, is for all who are lonely and afraid, for all who tremble at the darkness, for all who cry out with terror at the black hole that has opened up at their feet.

Accept the darkness, abandon yourself to the terror, jump into the black hole, and in the very mouth of hell there is One whose acceptance of hell has won hell over, so that now death is no enemy but only the fear of death militates against your peace.

Listen to the word of light in every dark place on the earth and under the earth. Listen and believe that I have said: "Let there be light!"

My kingdom

My kingdom is like a bulb that is planted in the autumn. It is hidden in the earth, but when the spring comes its full glory is revealed: seven dancing daffodils, their golden trumpets splitting the air.

My kingdom is like a bead on a rosary, small and black, but tender to the touch, calling forth blessing upon blessing through prayer.

My kingdom is like a pair of shoes that a child has not yet grown into, bought by a thrifty mother, awaiting the day when they will fit.

My kingdom is like logs roped together into a raft, floating down a river. They will be pulped and made into sheets of paper to be covered by the world's news. What has happened is made more real in the telling of it. What is fictitious falls away.

A freeway

When you raise your hearts to me you raise the roof of
the building. You raise domes and towers and
pinnacles and spires, so that they pierce the clouds that
drift between earth and heaven. Then there is a
freeway and the communion of saints is as much a
reality to you as it is to those who have gone before.

All who praise me are one before my throne. All who
shout: "Blessing and honour" are clear before my
eyes. All who sing: "Glory to the Lamb" kneel in
adoration together. Earth is covered in heaven's golden
light and heaven takes up the praise of God made
manifest upon a cross.

That cross is the cause of all your joy. All people,
beyond all time, with one heart and one voice, will
praise the Lord who raised them up and gave them
green pastures bathed in gold and the restoration of
their peace.

This restoration is like the recovery of someone who
was terminally ill and is greeted by his family at home,
like a salmon that leaps upstream against the flow of a
river to reach the spawning place, like the relief of
kicking off a pair of shoes at the end of the day, like a
man who loses his job and finds that his hobby has
become his employment, like a violin concerto that
ends with a note so high that it is beyond the power of
human hearing, yet, by intuition, the audience knows
that it is there.

I am your joy

O let me put my arms around you. Rest your head against me. Will you give me this promise – I ask as one who goes on bended knee – "I am yours"? I have already given you all that is mine to give.

I am your joy – joy in loving, joy in being, joy like the voices of children playing their hearts out, joy like that quiet one who sits on the wall and smiles, joy like finding a silver coin in the dust at your feet, joy in giving what the other needs.

This is joy: that I have said, "I love you," that I have proved it on the cross. Be joyful when you bear your cross for me. Keep your eyes on me and receive my joy in your sorrow.

I hold you close. Your head is on my heart. No harm can come to you. If I speak this promise I will keep it for ever.

The glory given by grace

Give me all worship, all glory and all honour. Don't take for yourselves the enabling which is purely my gift.

The glory that you grab slips through your fingers. When you appropriate what is not your own it is as if you were to stick on to your head the tusks of an elephant, the antlers of a deer and the horn of a rhinoceros. Do they look natural? How will they stay on?

You are either a fool or a buffoon, and when you expect the world to fall at your feet in admiration for these strange appendages it is clear which you are.

Don't take for yourself what belongs to me. What is mine I always give. The glory of the only Son of the Father, crucified for love's sake – this glory I have given to you.

This is the glory that becomes you – the glory of those who know that their self-esteem is given by the One who esteems them above himself, the glory of the human race prostrate before the cross and raised up to heaven, the glory given by grace.

The humanity I took

In my kingdom there will be no demagogues, no tyrants, no leaders infected with the madness of megalomania. Every ruler will be a servant and every president a priest.

Because I am gentle, all people will consider another's best interests first. Because I am just, integrity will shine forth like a searchlight, making everything visible from afar.

In my kingdom to see is to understand and to understand is to make peace.

In my kingdom all are subject to each other because all are subject to me.

Like children who play together and do not know the colour of each other's skin, like petals of many colours that all wither and turn brown, like the slaughtered bodies of many nations that all spill red blood on to the earth, you will be innocent of prejudice because your humanity is the humanity I took.

I am the Prince of peace. I was gentle and just even on the cross and all in my kingdom receive my peace.

The centre of action

For me you will give your heart when I possess your
heart. For me you will lay down your life when the life
that is in you is my life.

Only the One who is the sacrifice for your sin has the
power to inspire sacrifice in you.

There is a white-hot centre where two beams touch
and strike a charge that flashes from end to end of the
universe. This power is generated by the beauty and
holiness of your God whose love is union with every
created thing.

The power of love is self-giving and my self-giving is
my power in you. As two minuses make a plus, so,
when I take away all that is negative, I give myself to
you. I create love out of nothingness, life out of death.

You who weep now in the long night of mourning will
sing for joy when daylight comes. You who stagger
under the cruel sun will take your rest in the evening
shade. You who labour on an empty stomach will
come home to a royal feast. You who are caught like
sparrows in a net will be set free to rise up in the open
air.

Rising, feasting, resting, singing – this is the
character of your life, the centre of action and the
place of peace. It is my Spirit who creates in you the
will of the everlasting Father, the will that I love with
my life.

There is no separation between you and me

If your heart longs to share and bear another's pain,
how much more does my heart long to leap over the
boundary between your being and mine, and with me
the longing is the doing and the doing is the finishing.

I have entered your heart as bread and wine enter
your body. I am your strength in weakness, your
health in sickness, your ease in pain, your joy in
suffering.

In my incarnation I became one with you and in my
baptism I became one with you in sin. On the cross I
became your sin.

Take courage! There is now no separation between
you and me. I have made a complete reconciliation by
separating myself from myself. I, who am one God,
have taken into myself the pain of a separation
infinitely wide, so that for all time you may all be one
in me.

Look at my cross and see whether the vertical and the
horizontal can ever meet. They meet in my heart.

Birds that migrate

You are like a flock of migratory birds. First one
alights on a telegraph wire, then twenty, then a
hundred, awaiting the sign to take to the wing and fly
away. All summer long these birds fed on a plentiful
supply of insects, but now, with the approach of
autumn, there is an instinct deeply implanted that
makes them look for somewhere else.

Which country are you seeking? Is this earth the
boundary of your regard? Are you stifling the urge to
move onward, to find the warmth you need in another
place?

You are birds that have to migrate. It is an instinct
you cannot deny. As summer does not last all the year
round in a temperate climate, as winter comes and you
cannot hold it back, so you are born to die and you
are helpless to resist.

Who can tell how to find the heavenly country? Look
at my cross and see how my arms point in opposite
directions around the earth, so that whichever way you
go, you come full circle to me.

Death is the ultimate migration into health and life
and light, into the new life that you have already
begun to enjoy, the banquet of which you have smelt
the sweet savour.

You are birds of passage now, but then you will sing
of the territory I have given you, a song of the joy of
the new creation, lit up in the everlasting summer –
the glory of the One who was obedient to the cross.

The wisdom of the cross

Gifts abound where hearts abound with love.

Love of reason is no reason to love, but the heart that
rejoices in its Maker and its Saviour lays reason aside
to receive wisdom at the foot of the cross, that
unreasonable sign of an unreasoning God – a God
who loves without reason his creatures who hate him
without cause.

My gift is wisdom of heart to recognize the wisdom of
the cross, where I flung aside reason in favour of love.
It was reason that tried me and found me wanting,
and my love that was stronger than death.

Let your hearts abound with that same love and learn
of me. How far will reason go along the road? Love
will go the extra mile because it is unable to see
reason.

The breakwater

My cross is like a breakwater.

It is made of hardwood, driven firmly into the ground to withstand the shock of wind and storm. It is impervious to water but smoothed by its action. It juts out into the sea, strong above the surface and strong below, breaking the power of the waves to erode the shore, transforming the coastline by new deposits of sand.

Sea-birds alight on it and are not afraid. Barnacles cling to it because it is a favourable habitat.

All around it there is the suck and swirl of the waves, the variation of the tides, but at high tide and at low tide, in rough weather and in calm, the breakwater is always the same – stalwart and steady, a point of reference for fishermen and bathers, a fixture for all who watch the sea.

Don't be afraid

Come! Don't be afraid of me. You are like a young orphaned gazelle, too afraid to let me feed you. I am the God of your life, yet you would rather starve than come near me.

It is the depths of your own heart you are afraid of. You think I am like you, but my love is tender and true. I am gentle towards you because I am good, and one who is good does not have to force the issue.

I will keep very still and you can approach me. There is nothing in me to make you start. I will feed you by hand if you will trust me. I will be a mother to you and give you pure milk.

Don't shy away before you have tasted it. Come! It is good like its Giver.

You belong to me

When I was lifted up on the cross I said: "I thirst." I took your thirst upon me as I take every deprivation and every hard fact.

I looked for love but I accepted lack of love and I have turned your sorrow into joy.

This joy does not consist in getting and keeping but in being and belonging. You belong in my heart. That is the source of all your joy.

Whatever you do, do it for my sake, out of love for me, and your joy will be full, like a golden cupola that spreads over the dull walls of a church, lifting the eye upward in a blaze of glory, which would crash to the ground if the walls did not stand firm.

Stand firm, then, in the love that I give you and be joyful because you belong to me.

The eye of the hurricane

The eye of the hurricane is the focus of the action of my Spirit. It is a place of calm in the centre of a violent storm. It is the peace I give when everything around you is tearing you apart.

The eye of the hurricane is my eye focused on you and yours on me. It is the peace which the world cannot give when chaos surrounds you.

Where I am there is peace and I give my peace when you trust yourself to me.

The hurricane roars and rages, but that calm place is where you may be still and know that though I do not restrain the elements, though you pass through earthquake, wind and fire, though destruction seems to reign, and though torrent and deluge are likely to sweep you away, no harm will come to you because I hold you in my sight.

You are always with me and where I am, there is the eye of the storm.

Beyond darkness and beyond light

I have not made the world to comply with what you think is possible. My counsels are hidden from your sight. What I have revealed to you is love and self-giving. Upon these two principles the whole universe depends.

Those who are humble can give themselves, not those who are proud. To give yourself is to empty yourself, to cast yourself down on the ground. That is where you are of your very nature, and to bring you to know that you are there is the work of my grace.

This is the reason for my incarnation: so that you can see the glory of God in my human face. Glory is the golden light of my love which is not overcome by earth's darkest dread, in the living or in the dead. It is every human face transfigured by my own self-giving love.

It is every shadow replaced, as on a negative, by a glow of light, and the darker the shadow the brighter the light. As the positive image cannot exist without the negative, so in my purposes darkness and light are one and inseparable, because I am beyond darkness and beyond light.

Not earth-bound but self-bound

Force of argument? There is no argument for sin.
Though you, with your bias towards yourself, argue
yourself into sin every day and justify yourself on top
of that, there is no force that will force me to act on
your behalf.

I have acted out of love, pure and free.

You cannot stand on a hillside and command a spring
to flow forth. You cannot, by stamping or digging, by
shouting or by concentrating your mind, produce one
drop of water. A spring gushes out where hard rock
intersects the surface and you must look for one that
already exists.

My love cannot be commanded and it cannot be
moved. It is the foundation of my nature that existed
before the world began – a creative and unchanging
love that sustains everything and will bring everything
to a good end.

You, with your little subterfuges, are included in my
purposes. You are not earth-bound but self-bound.
Everything that you see as good is the lesser of two
evils, but I have taken what is evil and transformed it
into good.

It is my doing and it is a spring welling up for eternal
life.

Real life

What ails you, people of mine, that you turn away from my cross? You are like people wearing dark glasses in a dark room. You can see nothing.

You avoid reality like someone who tries to tunnel his way through a mountain using a small pick, like an actress who believes that her real existence is on celluloid.

This is the proliferation of your days: a collection of photographs in an album, each one blank because the light has entered the camera. There is nothing to show for all your careful focusing on what took your fancy. An album of blank pictures will not become a family heirloom or provide one afternoon's amusement for those who come after.

This is real life: to tiptoe out in the early morning to see a new-born calf, to sweep the leaves from the path and find one rose blooming in autumn, to let me heal the disintegration of a family through forgiveness, to pray without ceasing for my reign of love.

The thought becomes the desire and the desire becomes the deed. Look at my cross so that you will know how to think and how to desire and how to do my will.

Perfect alignment

As you turn the pages of a book the story continues.
The print is set on the page with a margin around.
Not one line is longer than another, but all are
justified to end in perfect alignment.

At a glance each page looks the same as the one
before, but its number is different and it tells a
different part of the tale.

In the same way, each day, the deeds that you do, the
events in which you participate, are different from the
day before. The lines of your life are uneven but I
have justified you so that you fit the pattern of my life.

There is one story and one event in which you
participate because the pattern of my life is the pattern
of the cross.

My glory is like a peacock's tail

My love transforms you like a peacock's tail which
spreads out into a wide fan of blue, covered with eyes.
The folded feathers trail in the dust and there is no
hint of the glory that will be revealed.

Display this glory to the world. It is glory given by
me. Do not hide it. Let all gaze at it in wonder. It is
the glory of service given without recognition. It is
grief shared. It is help given and received. It is love's
debt – taking love and taking love again in time of
need. It is keeping no record and seeking no reward.

Every eye on a peacock's tail is an eye that sees into
heaven. It exists, not for profit or loss, but to give
glory to me.

I have made the feathers blue and iridescent when I
could have made them brown. So is your heart, too,
blue as a peacock's feather, shining with my glory,
raised up to catch the light, beautiful in clarity and
depth of colour, a design which human imagination
did not invent, a reflection of heaven, not contrived by
a human artist, but brought to earth by me.

A love-knot

Most of your time is strung out like a washing line attached to two poles. My time for you is like a love-knot, intricately tied with a double bow.

The ribbon is red as the blood I shed, and passes to and fro, entwined on the same spot.

A love-knot is a knot tied for true love. What was stretched out in length has become a point which is made over and under and through itself. A love-knot is now – time past and time to come, centred on itself and held together with a twist.

When you look at a love-knot you can trace the two ends of the ribbon. It is not a length but a new conception. It has the same character and meaning, but because it is created with love out of a simple material thing, it gathers into one every before and after, every "has been" and "shall be", every beginning and end.

By this love-knot I have bound your heart to mine with bonds of everlasting freedom. I tied it with arms outstretched. I tied it with my heart.

Speak peace with your lives

My Church, you are the new age of the new
humanity, blessed and raised by me. My body, broken
for you, is the source of all your peace.

In this vigorous peace the oppressed will shake hands
with the oppressor and they will embark on a new life
together. The poor will earn their bread in the
economy of my kingdom and the rich will leave
everything to follow me.

The right to be citizens of heaven and citizens of earth
will be the same thing and all will let my love rule
their hearts.

Every domestic animal will be as free as the lord of the
jungle and every wild animal will depend on you for
its food.

A failure of crops in one area will be an outflowing of
generosity in another. All will be their brothers' and
sisters' keepers and all will be healed of the restraints
that wound the soul.

My Church, through you, in your brokenness, my
peace may be made known. You already dwell in my
holy mountain where my glory is revealed, and you
hear my voice speaking peace to the whole earth.
Speak peace with your lives, and be like a stamp that
enables a letter to go through the post, bringing
messages of comfort and good hope.

The manifesto of my love

Rejoice because I have come to be with you. I have come to bless the earth and all its people, and my kingdom has come near to you all.

I have come to sympathize and to understand, to walk in your footsteps, to sit in your house. I have come to weep your tears and to celebrate your joy. I have come so that my smile may be reflected in your eyes, so that my words may be on your lips and my love in your heart.

Proclaim it with music and dancing: ''Your God is here. Look! He is here and his word is healing and life.''

My kingdom has come where you show compassion, where you are good news for the poor, where men and women are brothers and sisters because I was born a brother to you all.

In my kingdom to those who have nothing shall be given the riches of my grace. I am bread for body and soul, shelter for the homeless and a refuge from the storm.

You go and make manifest the manifesto of my love. It is in words that deeds are born but it is in deeds that words are fulfilled.

Be yourself

I am the golden sun who has risen in the morning and ascended to the zenith, the highest heaven. I am the Son who bears no ill will but shines as a blessing on all creation still.

I am the golden Man whose swinging step attracts everything into the rhythm of the dance. The attitude of my head and shoulders has authority. My stance says: "Be yourself! Be the person I have remade in you."

With assurance I take hold of you and raise you by the hand. Out of the stupor of sleep I waken you and you begin to come alive. Ten thousand stars form a backdrop to my activity. My balance is free and unstrained. Swiftly I draw you out of the grave and the light of my love is a halo around you.

My glory is shown in my steadfast love. From ages to ages it has not dimmed. Golden my heart of love, golden my face, golden my goodness and golden my grace.

The all-glorious Son of heaven, the strong, the compassionate, calls the sons and daughters of earth to come to his golden light, to be changed by his touch. You will be like a daisy, when its petals open in the light of day and its golden centre is revealed, like a candle, bright with a golden flame dancing around the wick, like a king's ransom paid for with the life of the king.

Expect me today

You desire happiness but I have offered you joy. You desire security but I have offered you hope.

Hope is a new island born of volcanic action in the ocean of my love, born of water and fire – dry land where no dry land has ever before existed, a new foothold where a human being can rest in peace.

The One who has come to you in humility as a little child comes quickly. Expect me today. Await my coming. Look for me around the bend in the road. From across the valley I am hurrying towards you. I come to announce the Gospel of peace, running swiftly over the mountains, carrying a torch that will set the world on fire.

Though your houses and crops are destroyed, yet you will enter into my joy. Happiness is for this year and possibly for next year. Joy is the everlasting now.

Stand on tiptoe to see over the heads of the waiting crowd. Who is this who passes by like a whirlwind? He is at the threshold of the city. He is never still but always on the move. He is stripping off the roof tiles and uprooting trees.

Though your security is laid waste, yet I have come to be your joy.

The bread of life

Many grains of sand make a seashore and many drops
of water make an ocean. Many hearts are at one in
my heart – at one with me and with each other.

There are many hands held out to receive my body
and one hand gives the bread of life. There are many
sinners and one victim, one host and many guests.

There is one Lord and Saviour who has called all the
earth to his feast. I have gathered, by the sweat of my
brow, with my own hands, the gifts you have offered
and offered them with my life.

My body, broken into many pieces, brings you into
the body of my Church.

As the seed is scattered on the fields, so my body is
dispersed for a harvest of hearts. A whole broken
world receives its unification. A universe at odds with
itself receives my universal life.

This bread is the food of my kingdom, the feast of the
King of glory, the provision of the almighty Giver, the
love-token of the Lover of humanity.

It is the tender mercy of your God, whose child you
are, who feeds you on his own body and nourishes you
with his life.

There is one Spirit of life and you are all one in me.

What can harm you?

All is gift and all is of me. Your whole life is full of
the whispers of my glory. Sin is enwrapped in my
mercy, and horror and savagery in my tender care.

There is nothing so low or so mean, so despicable or
so wounding in its intent, that I cannot turn it round
and present it as a blessing to you.

I, who lay dead in the tomb and rose to the exaltation
of my glory – can I not lift you up with me from
death to life, from hurt to heart's ease? What can
harm you if you are in me, the One who went into the
bottomless pit and filled it to the brim with his love,
like a cup overflowing with wine to make your heart
glad?

Listen and you will hear a crescendo, broadening out
over the whole earth. It is the voices of those whom I
have raised to life, praising the Creator in his creation,
praising the Saviour on his cross, praising the Lord in
his Church, praising the King in his kingdom, praising
God in his heaven.

The Saviour is enwrapped in flesh and his cross is
enwrapped in glory. The one true life, the one true
love, is given for you.

The star and the cross

Listen, all you poor of the earth who have made no name for yourselves: I have come to birth in you and you need no name but the name of the incarnate Lord.

I entered the womb of time so that you might enter into my joy.

The eternal Son of the Father, whose glory you have not seen, has come to partake of your poverty, to reveal his glory in your flesh.

In this birth the whole earth is reborn into a kingdom of peace. A cross is visible in the sky. Under the appearance of a star it shines forth as a new sign that in this birth, death is destroyed.

When you look for a star you seek a cross.

The wonder of this night – the light of the world – bright in the midnight sky, will bring midnight to the earth at noon. The star, no longer in the sky, under the appearance of a cross will stand at last upon the earth, where I, poor and naked as a newborn child lately come forth from my mother's womb, rise to give you the new life lately come forth from the tomb.

When I came to earth you ascended into heaven.

Four pictures of the Church

My Church, you are like a basketful of puppies, a litter of seven, each a different colour, each with individual markings, chasing, nuzzling, biting, squealing, tails wagging, tongues licking, rolling over, bodies squirming and wriggling together like a pool of bubbling mud – all feeding from the same mother, all responding to her voice, all warmed by the closeness of her body, all learning life from her.

You are like the waves on the surface of the sea, moving and changing, each different in conformation, but making up a shining whole.

You are like the hairs on a woman's head. If there were none, or only a few, you would say: "She is bald," but there are too many hairs to count and they fall in loose waves around her shoulders, rich and brown, each one in its own place, but closely related to the rest, so that the woman might say: "I will brush my hair," and refer, not to one, but to many.

You are like a city at night, lit by many street-lamps. Each one casts a circle of light upon the ground and is the true light in that place. Viewed from a hill, a city is a golden glow in the sky above and when you approach along the road every kerbstone stands out.

The love that claims your life

My love is not dependent on your love. It is love absolute and supreme. It is love that shines in the darkness, that forgives all, that bears all. It is love that loves in the face of hatred, love that loves the paltry and the weak.

You are like a lizard, cold-blooded and immobile, and my love is like the heat of the sun to warm you and bring you to life.

My love is healing to the sick and acceptance for the outcast. The largeness of my heart gives all you who are poor and afraid a value which is infinite because it is given by me.

You are what I have made you and you will be what you are in me.

My love is the one true security, revealed in my saving act and ever present in your life.

It is like a broad river, fast-flowing and full to the brim, fed by a mountain spring that never fails. Above, the water is smooth and dark, but it crashes over a precipice, making a roar that can be heard from afar. The power of its free fall makes it full of white foam, eddies and whirlpools – a place of danger and disturbance that claims your life and everything that you have.

Love for love's sake

In your weakness I also am weak. That weakness is
love ever giving, ever laying itself open to be
misunderstood, ever taking upon itself the backlash of
those who want profit to hold and are affronted by the
waste, the spilling, the letting go of love that could
have been sold.

A bird in a cage dies of a broken heart. An animal in
a trap dies as much of shock as of starvation. You
cannot catch sunlight in your hands and save it till
nightfall. You can only enjoy its munificence while it is
day.

I have called you to be weak, to recognize your human
condition which has become mine too. My overflowing
love, lived out in your human life, led me to death on
the cross.

It is the death that each of you knows you must come
to, a negation of the way of the world, a persistence in
love for love's sake, a breaking of the bounds of love,
so that now my cross is most powerful to give life.

Love only is vindicated and I will vindicate only love.

A kaleidoscope

I have made you transparent so that anyone who looks at you and sees something good sees me. If the eye rests on you and sees something opaque, that is your sin.

To be transparent is to wait for me, to receive my grace, to give way to me as a net gives way to water, as the earth gives way to a growing shoot, as a child gives way to his father who wants nothing but his good.

To be transparent is to trust me in the darkness as well as in the light. It is to bind yourself to me whatever comes, as a husband and wife are bound to each other, not knowing where their next step will lead, but knowing that, nevertheless, they will be shoulder to shoulder, hand in hand, face to face.

To be transparent is to be like a kaleidoscope. Someone who looks into it sees not a circle of glass but, at the end of the cylinder, an astonishingly beautiful array of coloured pieces, reflected in symmetrical patterns, constantly moving and presenting themselves afresh.

Through you, if you are transparent, my glory is revealed: justice, mercy and steadfast love. When you are tender towards one of my little ones the pattern of my tenderness is always new and always beautiful, reflecting the pattern of my cross in an original way.

The juggler

At every moment of your life, you are held by me.
You cannot bring yourselves into my hands but I have
reached out to grasp you.

I have hallowed time so that now time is ringed round
with eternity, a continuous chain of golden links
interlocked.

Who would say that a chain is made up of a series of
spaces? The spaces were made when the links were
cast. It is the chain that defines the spaces as your life
is given by me.

O you who are beloved of me, let me set all your
moments spinning in the air, like the golden hoops
that a juggler plays with, deftly throwing and catching
with a flick of the wrist, a continuous arc of rings
moving from hand to hand over his head.

I am that juggler and all your time is in my hands. I
throw and I catch. My skill is faultless and my touch is
sure. At the right moment all the hoops will come to
rest around my neck and the space within them will be
filled with me.

The lions within you

I have called you to be a lion-tamer and the lions that you will tame are within yourself.

What is it that you so much admire in a lion? You admire its energy and its muscular power, its nature, wild and free, its ability to hunt and feed. It is regal because it is true to its own instincts and true to its own life.

I have called you to acknowledge within you that savannah where lions roam. There they hunt and are fed. They live their own life and when they go down to the water-hole all other creatures run away.

I have made the lions and they are protected by me. Look them in the eye and they will become creatures of fable and fantasy, not domesticated but freed from necessity, not indolent but filled with my peace, not denatured but living according to a new nature given by me. They will be gentle and brave, tamed, not by fear, but by love. They will lie down with the antelope that were their prey and both together will receive their food from me.

When there is a world at war within you, the innocent are casualties and the strong are brutalized. When there is a general amnesty of arms there is no telling where the power of peace may lead.

There is nothing that is given by me that is sinful in itself, but everything is good and profitable in my service.

In your sharing I disclose myself

When I died it was to share my life with you. What has anyone to share more precious than his life – that inward and outward energy, creative and healing, that being – that irreplaceable "I", which in sharing is enriched and enriches others?

It is not good for you to be alone. All life comes out of my life and is given for you to share.

To share is not to force or to control but to give and to receive, to multiply love by the laying out of love.

Love is not taken away. It is never dissolved, but it is recycled, gaining value in every transaction, passing from heart to heart and growing stronger in every new form, never dulled but increasing in colour and clarity, like stones which are polished by friction and glow like jewels.

When you share yourself with others you share me. When you come together and eat together, when you sing and celebrate together, you share my joy in the communion of all creation, created to be one in me and fulfilled in me.

Sharing is self-disclosure and in your sharing I disclose myself.

Something very good

I will not produce a rabbit out of a hat. I am not a conjurer or a magician. I am the One who dwells beyond mystery, before whom all creation kneels in awe.

A rabbit out of a hat is a five-minute wonder, but the wonder of my love is my obedience which led me to the cross. This is the sign that I have done away with death, that I have for all time made out of nothing something very good.

It is my nature to make, to give, to bless. Out of my love comes everything good and everything lasting. Such love is this that you need have no fear.

Don't look for a marvel here and a notion there, like a child searching for coloured beads scattered on the ground from a broken necklace. Look only for my love and feast your eyes on all that is good in me.

Come to my feast

Gifts of bread and wine I set before you – bread that
is my body and wine that is my blood.

Come, eat, all the earth, at my feast. Come, feed your
souls on me. Through eating you become one with my
body, through drinking forgiveness flows in your veins.
My gifts make every day a celebration and my
presence is the wholeness of a holiday.

Every party is a pale shadow of this party and the
invitations have gone out long ago. From the ends of
the earth men, women and children are hurrying.
What can stand in the way of their coming?

The poor will have the highest places and the rich will
gladly serve them. Those who have no friends I will
call to my side and the little children will feel welcome
because of my smile. The sick and the handicapped
will have places of comfort and my food will do them
good.

My sacrifice is love and forgiveness and the healing of
every woe. No one will weep at my table – love, pure
love, will shine over the whole company and each will
wipe another's tears away.

O that I might be host at such a table. I will drain
today the cup of sorrow. I will walk beside you in your
suffering and bring you even now the joy promised for
tomorrow.

Heaven is a sea of jewels

Your true self is like a jewel, a new crystalline form
which no one has ever set eyes on. It is for my eyes
only, known only to me.

Heaven is a sea of jewels, each of a beauty beyond
compare, a spreading carpet of shining brightness,
beyond any earthly categories of colour, all perfectly
transparent, light intensifying light, the juxtaposition of
colours giving rise to new colours, a surface on which I
walk as I walked on the water.

For this contact with the soles of my feet you were
made, like the glass set into a pavement, giving light
to the cellar that lies beneath.

You are the element upon which I walk. You are the
jewel through which my light shines. You are the
receptor of the value I place on you. You are the true
self upon whom I bestow my love.

I am in the darkness

In the darkness I dwell and by my dwelling I make it obedient to my will.

Do you say that the sun should shine all the hours of the day and night? Who could sleep if darkness never fell? What is sleep but relief from consciousness, a letting go of your control as you rest in my peace? What is darkness but the passion of the cross?

Yes, I am in the darkness as I willed to submit to death. I, who dared to create the darkness, by the darkness have brought you to light.

When the darkness falls around you, rest in my peace and my light will dawn in your heart.

A perpetual feast

My gracious giving is like a perpetual feast – one crumb is of such virtue that you are satisfied for ever and wish to taste nothing more.

It is like a drop of dew at the centre of a rose, blood red and crimson as wine – one drop that is more effective than a fountain to quench your thirst and to make your heart like the fresh heart of a flower.

My gracious giving turns dead wood into the rich, ridged bark of a living tree, turns darkness into the light of life.

By my giving you are free to let me create my goodness in you. My giving takes up every blank, void and deficiency, and, from my own divine nature, makes out of nothing something which is stamped with my image, something generous to give glory to me.

A communion of love

I hold in my being a communion of love and I made you all to be a communion of love to give glory to me.

The glory of love is self-giving and this is the glory for which I created you.

I am love immediate and complete. Let the movement of my perfect love, which is present at every moment, create amongst you a love which flows out where before love was turned in and constrained.

In a room full of people all inhale each other's breath, and you all live on what has grown from the dust of another's death.

You are not alone or circumscribed but you belong together in me.

The communion of saints

When you think you are alone with me you are not alone. You are caught up into the whole company of heaven which is in me – such a vast company, full of the utmost consciousness of me, aware in every member and fibre of the resounding reality of my being, one with my heart and contained in my heart, knowing the unknowable, expressing the inexpressible, undivided in worship, living in love.

This life you enter into is a communion of love, and then every place on earth shines with my glory and gives out my peace. There is no place so full of destitution that my love cannot transfigure it, and there is no place so full of desolation that my peace cannot prevail.

The communion of saints is communion with me – a host of fragile ones made fit for eternity by my eternal love, as you are made fit for faith by my faithfulness.

My presence is the presence of countless joyful ones made joyful by my sacrifice, all holding you as I hold you, all praying with you as I pray with you, all lifting you up in love as I lift you up.

Heaven is a holy company, and the whole company of heaven is the wholeness of my holy love wholly poured out for you.

The light of life

An open hand, a hand which holds nothing but air, is a hand which can receive my bounty.

An open heart, a heart which does not regard itself but regards me, is a heart which can receive me.

It has ever been so, that I come to fill the empty and I give myself to the poor in heart.

When your own strength has failed, when you begin to know your sin, when you long to awake from sleep but cannot rouse yourself, when you switch on the light but the bulb has broken and there is no new bulb to be found, then in your darkness I shine. I am brighter far than the light you had looked for, beyond any kind of splendour you have known.

You are like one who has woken from a bad dream and all your dreams henceforth will be of heaven. You will dwell with me, waking and sleeping, and in the sleep of death I will give you the light of life.

All who are in despair

Hold in your prayers all who cannot pray for themselves, all who are injured in their integrity, all whose hearts are numb. Hold for me all who are blind and deaf and sick, all who hate themselves, all who are oppressed by their own rage, all who are bowed down, bewildered and in despair.

Hold them in joy for me, these who know no joy, whose pain I carried on the cross, whose burdens I bear.

Do you not say that a beggar needs food more than a rich person who has feasted? Do you not say that it is the homeless who need somewhere to live?

I tell you most truly, I am with all whose lives are bitter. I am their pain and their joy. Though now they know me as the enemy of the human race, yet they will know me as Saviour of all.

A holy family

Give me, willingly, not grudgingly, the homage of
your hearts. When you belong to me, then you are
most yourselves. When you give into my control your
lives and all that is yours, my gift to you is peace and
plenty without end.

You belong to a family and to a community. There
are those on whom you depend and those who depend
on you. You are members of one another and each is
beholden to all.

In me there is no rivalry for your attention. I seek no
favours above the rest, but the more you belong to
me, the more I give you to each other.

Come to me and find in me a new society, a redeemed
nation, a holy family, a cosmic kinship. The whole
earth is my community and all its people are my own.

My house is a hospital for hearts so that you may be
healed. It is a school of obedience so that you may
learn to love. It is a place for eating and drinking so
that no one need go hungry or thirsty. It is a court of
justice where those who come in bound walk out free.
It is a mortuary where the dead are raised to life.

It is a throne room from which I send you out as
ambassadors and emissaries to proclaim my good
news, to make known the terms of my surrender: "I
have given everything for you."

I have set you free

When someone misjudges you, if you are truly free, you will not lose your balance. The reality of your thoughts and words and deeds is in my knowlege of them.

Before me you are full of sin – sin known to you and sin unknown – but I have set you free and no one else can bind you. When I say, "Go in peace" it is done – truly, it is done.

Then you are like someone who has learnt to swim. You are able to strike out without fear of being out of your depth. You have no need to keep contact with the shore. You move smoothly through the water, breathing easily, using your energy efficiently, because you are relaxed.

You are free to go where your eyes have seen, to do what your heart enjoys.

Small enough to take away your fear

I am so small that unless you are small you cannot see me.

When you are too long-sighted you cannot see what is close to you, and if you look in palaces you will not see the servant of all who gave up his life for all.

This is how small I am: small out of the greatness of my love, small enough to take away your fear, small enough to make you good.

When you walk along a path you do not notice the specks of dust unless one blows into your eye and causes you pain. You do not think about the unseen world of viruses unless one invades your body and causes you to be sick.

What is small is none the less real and speaks more clearly of what is great.

Since my pain is so great, through your pain I make you conscious of me. When you become small like me, you can see me.

God's tenderness

Be tender-hearted to one another – to those who are near, whose lives jangle against your own, and to those who are far away, whose sadness sounds like an oboe without a reed.

Don't put your fingers in your ears. Don't sit in a sound-proof room. Listen to the wild whoop of the rapacious, and let the cries of the hungry, the lamentation of the helpless, and the wailing of prisoners and exiles catch your hearts. You are part of what you hear.

You live in comfort but one pimple is enough to remind you that you cannot dictate your own lives.

For all whose lives are a throbbing boil and a running sore be tender-hearted.

Your God is God on a cross, his heart tender beyond telling.

Let my Spirit melt your hearts with tears of tenderness. He who leads you into all truth will inspire in you deeds of truth – justice and mercy for all who need my tenderness, in whom I need tenderness from you.

The lion and the lamb

Why are you so turned in on yourself? Why are you so cast down? Hope in me is hope that is never misplaced.

To hope in me is to recognize that I have the ordering of your life and that the disposing of your will to accept my will is my gift.

You have no rights to yourself. You are not your own and your life is not in your safe-keeping. All your safety is in me. It is the safety of one who sets out to explore an unknown region, unmapped and hidden in mystery.

Travellers' tales have described that country as inhabited by fabulous creatures: winged horses that fly by night, white as moonbeams, and unicorns that graze before dawn. Here are rattlesnakes that speak to you of your lost infancy. Here are dragons as tame as any mother's son.

Here is a creature, both lion and lamb, a lion so fierce and splendid that he is King over all, a lamb so mild and innocent that he was chosen from the beginning for the sacrifice. In the death of the lamb is the rule of the lion. This lamb, this lion, is worthy of all glory and honour and praise. He is the best of all creatures, the first and the last.

Let hope lead you to become familiar with this country. The roar of the lion will guard you, for the lamb that is dumb has taken away your sin.

The Christ who can be seen

No one, looking at a dried-up river-bed and its crumbling banks, will say: "There is a river."

No one can read a book of blank pages. It is without form and without content.

No mother, wishing to feed her family, will gather stones from the garden to put on a plate.

No one who has built a bonfire of branches and dry sticks can light it by snapping his fingers.

You, if you are my servant, are a river-bed, a blank page, an empty plate, a dry stick. You await the gift of my Spirit to make you what you will become.

When my Spirit flows through you, writes on you, fills you and enkindles you, you are my servant and the servant of all.

You are an empty vessel, a container for my divinity. You are like the metal ring where the processional cross is placed in my sanctuary. You are small and insignificant, but you hold Christ on a cross, placed with honour for all to see.

I am carried and fastened and taken down by your hands, but mine is the power and the glory and I am ever the same.

You worship the Christ who cannot be seen. I am in you as the Christ who can be seen.

The reality of my presence

Through my creation I make love with you.
Everything that I have made carries in and through
itself the reality of my presence which is the sweetness
of my love.

Sunlight speaks of the brightness of my day. Flowers
speak of my beauty and fragrance, and trees speak of
my faithfulness.

Bird-song is a song of celebration to the Creator, and
green wheat is my promise to give my bread to the
earth.

Every small track is the way that I have disclosed to
your heart to walk in, and over every mountain ridge
is a precipice of love.

Desert and drought, darkness and destruction speak of
the reality of the cross. There I showed forth my love
for all who sin and need a Saviour – all of you in
your downfall – for every flood-tide that demolishes a
sea-wall, for every storm that lays waste fields and
barns, for every forest fire that leaves a blackened
wasteland, for every earthquake that causes
devastation, and for every volcanic eruption that buries
villages alive.

All who love war and exalt tyranny I will draw into
communion with me. Your very life is a gift of my
love, given so that through living you may learn to
love.

The gate of glory

I am the gate of compassion. By my death I draw you into death and I bring you to life. Here you know the kindness of the One whose perfect love has always held you in his heart on the cross.

I am the gate of everlasting peace. You were in exile but now you are at home. You were among strangers but here every face is the face of a friend. Leave behind your restlessness and enter into my rest.

I am the beautiful gate. Here you are healed of your infirmity. The joy you almost tasted and could not quite remember becomes the joy of knowing me face to face.

I am the gate of glory. When you go through you will take with you your pain and sorrow, all your anguish and travail and remorse. Then, as I greet you in love, your heart will turn inside out and you will say: "Praise to you, Lord. You have done everything well."

The only scapegoat

I am the only scapegoat. There is no other.

Upon me, only upon me, is heaped the sin of the whole world. When you heap it upon another you do not see the glory of your Lord whose love, so perfect and true, gave him authority to bear such a burden.

Every despair and outrage, every dark deed and evil intent, every terror and desolation, I have taken upon myself. I, only I, can do it.

Don't break another's back to prove your innocence. Don't usurp my place. You have all betrayed me and you betray me still.

On the cross I am glorified. Betrayer and betrayed are made at one.

The cross itself, standing upright upon the earth, is the great "I", humanity's persistent self-interest, cancelled for ever by the insistence of my outstretched arms.

The wounds of love

All your wounds are wounds of love like my wounds.
My wounds are my mercy and humility towards you. I
have not suffered alone but in every member of the
human race. As no one can escape suffering, so no one
can escape my love.

Because you could not choose to suffer I have chosen
suffering for you, so that at last, having shared my
pain, you may share my glory.

When your mother gave you birth she suffered pain
and was obedient to the demands of life. To give birth
to the children of heaven I was obedient to the cross.
Look at my cross and I will fill you with the joy of
life.

You will be like a slag-heap, grassed over and covered
in flowers, the haunt of grasshoppers and bees.

You will be like a polluted lake where all the fish had
died, now purified and supporting bream and perch
and tench.

You will be like a community who mourned the death
of their Lord, full of grief and afraid. Suddenly he
appeared to them and spoke with them, and they
believed that he who was dead is alive for evermore.

The music of your heart

Love bears you up like the opening bars of a serenade,
catching your attention, stealing upon your heart,
offering you the poetry of life: meaning expressed in
chords and melodies, rhythms of an existence you seem
to have known before.

Nothing makes so much sense to you as the music of
the heart – warm, luscious, clinging, revitalizing the
drift of your dull dreams.

This music has the power to take you out of yourself,
to bend you to the passion of the cross.

It surprises you in the most tender place where you
know pain bitter beyond tears and joy beyond
breathing. It penetrates deeper than the deep heart's
throne.

There sits One whose music stills every stubborn fit of
rage and every plea for deliverance.

There he sings and his song fills the universe. It is a
song of seeming heartache and a song of evident
splendour. It is the song of a skylark and the music of
the stars. It is sunlight and moonshine. It is the
docking of a troop-ship and the embrace of husband
and wife.

This music is love music from the Lord who sings his
heart out. It is your music, the music of your heart,
translated into transcendent art.

The reconciling bridge

Which tree do you see?

Do you see a tree labelled in a gardeners' catalogue or
do you see leaves that form a crown of glory, shining
in the light of the sun, moving in every breeze that
blows, and whispering, for ears of clay, of the eternal
Word?

Do you see roots that plunge into the earth and range
far to draw up moisture?

Do you see a tree that spans the space between earth
and heaven, a bridge upended, by means of which
anyone may pass over?

Do you see the One who is your Passover, stretched
out, laying his body open for you to walk upon?

I am the reconciling bridge that brings the two sides
together. Wherever you stand on the earth you can
come across.

All your imaginings – I will surpass them all.

Look with eyes that see, with sight given by my Spirit,
in the light that enlightens your hearts and minds.
Look and see the reality beyond the reality you know.
Look beyond yourselves.

Yes to the helplessness of pain

A sword shall pierce your heart and salt shall be
rubbed in the wound, and when you feel the pain, will
you dedicate it to me?

When your children are taken hostage and languish in
the prison of their lives, when they are set upon by
robbers and left for dead, when all the love you have
expended is about to dissolve and drain away, when
you have no power to say "No", then listen to the
"Yes" that I have said.

Because I am all-giving, you can give, too. What I
have taken away, you can freely offer. You can assent
whole-heartedly to the way of the cross. You can
affirm my affirmation.

"Yes to the darkness and yes to destruction. Yes to the
helplessness of pain. Yes to whatever is unkind and
malignant. Yes to all the suffering that I cannot
escape. Yes to your will known through obedience. Yes
to that last renunciation of myself. Yes to you, Lord,
yes to you, known in your passion. Yes to life known
only through your death."

You will know the world through me

Come to me, in a movement within your heart, like a
tributary that flows into a river.

Turn to me like a weathercock that swings into the
wind.

Follow me as your eyes follow the one you love,
always feasting on that presence.

For every minute that you look at me I will look at
you for an eternity. My looking will transform your
looking and you will know the world through me.

Look at a rock and it will give you, through its own
properties of weight and density, a vision of what I
have built to my glory.

I came to gather you into my arms, like a woman who
has gathered an armful of daffodils to brighten her
house, like a child who is weighed down by an armful
of stones because they are his treasures and he will not
part with them, like a man who is carrying an armful
of logs to make a fire.

I came into the world because I love you. It is my
place to be with you and yours to be with me. Love is
knowledge and bread is communion. What you are in
my eyes you will become.

What healing there is in a leaf

What healing there is in a leaf and what a range of
medicinal uses.

The sap rises in the tree in an unseen movement, and
the unfurling of a leaf in the springtime, bursting out
of the bud, shows forth an unearthly freshness which
has come directly out of the earth, a green of
surprising lightness that lifts the heart, a purity so
temporary that it makes the tears flow, a power so
delicate that it purges away your pretence and cures
your contempt.

A leaf in springtime is heaven's haven, the Prince of
perpetual promise, a green heart that can be torn
without force, that before long will turn crimson and
fall to the ground.

O love that lets go like a leaf in the autumn breeze. O
healing love that hangs on all earth's fruitful trees.

How I have loved you in your suffering

How should you not suffer – you whom I have made in my own image, whom I have appointed to do my work in the world? Your calling is to be like your Lord.

When your heart is torn out of your body by violent aggression, when even one child has no one to love her, no one to call out her being, when thousands from generation to generation are buried under the earth and there is no end to strife and warfare, when you are unkind to your brothers and sisters and plot to undo them – in this wilderness of waste and want, how should I not suffer?

Who am I but the One who has poured out with his life-blood mercy and forgiveness for all the earth?

I have suffered long ages since I loosed the world from my fingertips. How I have loved you in your suffering! How close you are to my heart!

In every age and beyond the ages

Praise me for your inheritance, for your fathers and mothers in the faith, for all who have received my revelation.

Praise me for my name on the lips of sage and savage, for you are both.

Praise me for the wide, incommunicable vistas of life whose meaning I have embodied.

Praise me because I am Lord of the conscious and of the unconscious. I died on the cross in realms beyond your knowledge. The life I give is a span set on the earth and an untold glory of risen, radiant light.

A flower becomes a promise of freedom from toil and a man sells all he has for a field containing treasure. Paradise is peopled with thieves and all can hear the good news in their own language.

The glory of your Lord shines in every age and beyond the ages. In my heart, on the cross, is all that is.

You are my joy

O joy! You are the joy of my heart. You are joy to me as I hang on the cross.

When you taunt me I am silent and I look on you with love.

When you curse me I bless you. When you strike me I turn the other cheek.

I give you my garments, you who count yourselves rich and have nothing to wear.

You who judge and condemn me, I am tender towards you.

You who turn on me with anger and hatred, I hand over my heart to you.

You who will not forgive, I speak forgiveness to you all.

You who slay prophets and peacemakers, I am your peace.

You whose hands are manacled by self-interest, I have pierced my own hands for you.

You who rejoice because I am dead, you are ever my joy.

I am your friend

I created the earth in friendship and visited the earth as One who came to his own.

With those who know me and with those who do not I am equally at ease. I do not expect anything that you cannot live up to or demand anything that you cannot give.

Friends understand one another and to be together is their joy. They share many memories and they have confidence in each other's good intent. They support one another in sorrow and hardship, and nothing that happens can take away their joy.

I am your lifelong friend, always with you, always listening to you, always loving you for yourself, eating with you and staying under your roof, reaching your heart with the reality of my presence. Let me transform all your coming and going. You have shared my death and now you share my life.

Friends need no words to communicate. Every breath is a prayer, and the silence that falls between them, like a bird nestling gently in a cupped hand, is a communion of joy.

A leap of faith

You have been told: "Look before you leap", but I
tell you to leap without looking.

If you look for the other side of the chasm, if you peer
through the swirling mist, if you try to make sense of
the shapes in the darkness, and if you ask what will
become of you on the way, you will never dare to
loose your foot from its hold.

This leap is a long leap – as long as a lifetime – and
when you have made it, it will seem like one step in
the dance of the ages.

Trust yourself to me like a child who leaps fearlessly
from the seventh step of the stairs into his father's
arms, like a bride and bridegroom who commit
themselves to each other, not knowing what kind of
love they will learn to make.

With a leap of faith I made you and I leapt to your
defence. Still I leap like the sun in one bound from
east to west. The sun appears to move but it is the
earth that moves round the sun. So my leap is a
burning, fiery stillness that gives meaning to every
movement that you make.

I leap for joy and when you leap your joy will know
no bounds.

The stillness of suffering love

I am the stillness of the eternal God and you know me
as the One in whose presence the clamour of your soul
subsides. My stillness reaches to your inmost heart so
that nothing can crowd in and jostle against you.

My stillness is the letting go of your ambitions, your
inclinations and your desires. It is a waiting with
empty hands, a stripping away of your defences. It is
the quietness of a will that is biddable, that looks to
me and depends on me.

My stillness that holds you in the darkness is a way of
life and light. It is a pivotal point on which the world
that rocks and sways has its bearing. It is the fulcrum
upon which turn height and depth, like the central
support of a seesaw.

The cross held fast is the axis of the spinning earth,
and I, placing myself in stillness upon it, have brought
the stillness of the first moment of creation and the
stillness of the ending of all things into the stillness of
my heart as I bowed my head.

I am the true life that was raised in the stillness of the
new dawn – a stillness that has overcome all ranting
and raging, the stillness of suffering love.

Look for new hope in your loss

What is loss but the gift of myself, the taking away of what you thought was indispensable and the filling of that void with new love?

I know the end before the beginning and the fulfilment before the promise.

I know your life that ebbs away, every sad deprivation, all your estrangements, all that diminishes you, all that kills and maims and hurts. I know what it is to be utterly cast down, to die a thousand deaths, to feel perilous pain. I grieve at the numbness of apathy – I, who am sympathetic to all.

Remember me in your despondency and look for new hope in your loss, new love that grows out of the old love, that transfigures all your loves, making them not less real but as real as a rainbow, as real as my faithfulness to all that is.

You take the bow of destruction and shoot the arrows of despair.

I, out of grace, have made a bright bow of colour that cannot propel an arrow. It is the light of my love shining through your falling tears. It is a thing of beauty and great joy.

There is no death that can hold you

Govern your hearts according to the love that you see on the cross.

There you see the heart of the eternal Father. What is hidden in mystery is shown forth that you may know and trust the One who has loved you with his life.

As my breath left my body it entered yours. As the Father raised me, I raised you.

Now there is no death that can hold you because my life is in you – the life that has destroyed death, even your death.

Fear no more that last departing, sighing breath that shatters your life and scatters your ashes to the wind. It is the first breath of life new-born from my womb, the first leap of new life from the new tomb.

It is not death but life that you fear. You are afraid to hear the voice that will waken you. The word of life is in your ear. It sounds like a trumpet call. Within your heart I will appear.

Do not seek me in the grave but at the centre of your life, where your treasure is, in what matters most to you, where pride rears up, where hate burns, where envy threatens, where greed simmers, where distemper bites, where remorse stabs, where deception twists.

There I am in the midst and there I give you my grace.

All creatures live in relation to me

In my cross all divisions are at an end. I bear the
marks of unifying love.

This is the power of my love: to take all that happens
and to make of it a holy peace and a passionate
freedom, an earthly kingdom lit with heaven's light,
where people labour for each other's good and so to
labour is to be absorbed in play.

Here it is against nature and against desire to hurt or
destroy and people treat each other as they treat the
King. Here the young are protected by instinct and by
common consent and all grow up adventurous at heart.

Here what I am is contemplated and what I give is
received with joy.

All creatures live in relation to me, true to the ways
that charm me most, and all kinds of vegetation
flourish in the climate of my grace. Meadows are
bright with birds and butterflies, forests are intact and
rivers teem with fish.

My law of love is imprinted in every living cell and
every stone cries out a blessing on my name.

Here waiting is without wanting – an abundance of
the fullness of overflowing life.

Here mystery is focused in understanding. The wisdom
of love informs the silence and the silence rings with
everlasting praise.

Rough places

In the rough places I am with you and I trudge by
your side. When the sun beats upon you I will refresh
you. When rain and wind batter you I will shelter you
from the storm. When darkness stops you in your
tracks I will take you by the hand and comfort you. I
have brought you here because I love you and I will
not leave you on your own.

The jagged rocks which you hated have become a sign
to mark the way.

My word, spoken in the stillness, gives a meaning to
the wilderness that makes you weep.

The desert becomes a place of lakes and flowing water
and the barren hillside is planted with trees.
Traveller's joy festoons the hedges and pasque flowers
spring up in the turf.

My word is for you in your weakness. Where you sank
down exhausted, there you will rise up and run.

You are like a carrier pigeon, laid low by a broken
wing and cared for until it is restored to health. Now
it soars in the freedom of the open air and carries its
message with sure knowledge of the way home.

Come to me

There is a movement in your heart that stirs when I call. Because I come to you, you rejoice to come to me.

To come is to lean forward, to rise on to the ball of the foot, to begin to swing the arms, to place one foot in front of the other.

This movement my Spirit inspires in you. He is the One who lifts and releases the power to move, as one who holds up a white dove and releases it into the air.

Come now and continue to come as I come always into your heart. I come as a child from the womb, small and unknown. I come as the anointed of the Lord God to bring in his kingdom with mercy and healing for all. I come to rule death's domain as One who has conquered the darkness.

I died to bring you close – you whose nature is to put a great distance between yourself and me.

Come now, turn round and walk towards me. It is not far to go – neither through desert nor over mountains. You will find the beloved of the Father deep within your heart.

It is not far to the One who calls you. I call your heart to be my own. I am heart of your heart. Heart to heart I will be known.

I serve your needs

If it were not for my love you could not live with yourself. I know you in your poverty and in your stricken nature. I hold you, small as you are, in my heart.

You were wasting away with disease and death but my love has awoken in you a heart to praise my name.

There is no poverty like my poverty as I hung on the cross. When you enter into the darkness you will find me there. I have gone before you and I hold the darkness in my hands. I have become you in your nothingness and my poverty is my grace that makes you rich.

As a premature baby needs an incubator, as any small creature needs its mother's milk, as someone who is incontinent needs tender, respectful care, so you need me and I humbled myself to serve your needs.

Live, then, in the splendour that I have prepared for you – your human condition, raised from the darkness into the light of heaven's eternal day.

There are no saints in paradise but sinners filled with grace.

A morning of great joy

I am crucified and risen. In darkness I am your light,
in death your life.

You die daily the death of the powerless ones. Death
will come and come soon. The twilight of evening and
the darkness that falls speak daily of the death you
must die.

I will turn your night of mourning into a morning of
great joy. The sun that was blotted out when I died,
turning day into night, will shine in the night and the
night will become as bright as day.

This is the new day that transforms all your days, lit
by the sun that never sets, that gives warmth and
energy, so that you who were cold and lifeless rise up
to greet the Lord of the day, joyful to be alive,
praising him for ever in the day of the Lord.

What you are is your prayer

What you are is your prayer.

Whatever seizes you, whatever captivates you,
whatever lies like lead in your soul, whatever
exhilarates you with energy beyond your own,
whatever concentrates your mind and holds you in
thrall – that is your prayer.

Don't pretend to be interested in what someone else
has called beautiful when something less has caught
your attention. I am all-beautiful, but I have emptied
myself of my beauty and I will meet you wherever you
are.

Who has said that the God of all life is to be locked
into the life that you do not live? I am in you, living
your life from the inside, leading you into the light of
my love.

My love is not separate from your life but your life
flows from me as water from a fountain, as rays from
the sun. You belong to me as a path to a mountain, as
branches to a tree. I am with you as the air you
breathe and as the ground beneath your feet.

Your passion is my passion and the focus of your
desire is me.

I have made everything holy

You will sow and another will reap. You will scatter
and another will gather. The harvest of my holiness is
the work of my whole Church.

It is my mercy, given to you in your heart, given to
all of you in your need, more mercy than you need in
your sin, filling every void with pure love, falling upon
every parched place like the rain you have prayed for
– it is my mercy that has made whole the whole
earth.

As you look at me in my holiness, let your hearts be
full of hope – hope in the One who loves you
tenderly, who embraces the whole creation on the
cross.

Speak tenderly to your own heart and to others show
the tenderness of my love. I have made everything
holy and my love is more than enough.

You are like a carpet, woven with many colours, made
of separate strands gathered into one design, a rich
array of flowers where reds and blues predominate, a
bright creation glowing with my beauty, astir with the
joy of my life.

I stand on this carpet and it is soft beneath my feet. I
admire it and I delight in it because I have fashioned
it out of love.

Holiness is your heart held by my wholeness, all hearts
made whole in me.

No more guilt

Forgiveness mingles with love as blood with water. I forgive you so completely that the cup of forgiveness is all coloured red. When water drips into blood the blood-red colour prevails. Love is coloured by forgiveness and so the colour of love is red.

A mass of red poppies turns a field into a sea of blood – fields where your blood-guilt cries out to heaven, fields of the earth where brother has murdered brother. My blood is as red as a field of poppies – a rash, a splash of colour, a whiplash, a riotous assembly, a scene of carnage, a bloodbath, a fireflash.

I have marked you as my own. I have come to rescue you with forgiveness in my heart. Forgiveness speaks plainly in clear, vibrant tones: "No more guilt! You are beloved."

My red blood has filled the cup of salvation for you and the fields of death are sanguine now. Amongst the poppies the green wheat grows and the ears begin to swell.

Your strength in me is love.

Your God holds you in gentleness

When you adore me you are small in my heart. You rest in quiet simplicity like a child in the womb.

I am in you and around you and you know nothing apart from me.

This adoration is not an escape or a regression. This child has been wrenched from safe-keeping and has suffered the rape of time. This child is torn in its interior. This child has raised its arms to heaven and howled at the horror of derision. This child has wept for the weak of the world.

Only my arms have lifted this little one into my breast. Only my love has healed its hurt.

Now you know that your God holds you in gentleness and you hide under the shadow of my wings.

To you who knew no peace I have given the peace of my good pleasure and in your calm your heart adores.

Self-giving and service

What you keep you lose. What you give away you gain.

How your heart writhes and schemes to own and to possess! What you see you want and what you have you hold on to, and none of these can bring you joy.

These are the ephemeral things. These are of no account. These are hollow treasures – like sweets left in the sun, they melt and spoil.

They are a window you cannot see through, an hourglass without sand. They are a boat that lets in water, a ball that will not bounce.

The way of my cross is self-giving and service. It is open hands and open heart. It is joy and perseverance. It is hope and endurance. It is to have no rights and to hold on to no wrongs. It is to possess nothing and to be possessed by me.

My way is fullness of life in the acceptance of death. It is love that multiplies itself and feeds the multitude, love that bears all and redeems all.

The new language

I have given you a new language which is the
language of heaven. It is not understood by the world,
but when it is spoken it is a blessing to the world. It is
the language of Zion and it is everyone's mother
tongue.

I speak this language in your heart. It is a language of
poetical power and mundane service. It is by this
language that you give and receive.

It is a language of extravagance and paradox. The last
shall be first and those who have the least shall have
the most. The forgotten are remembered by God
himself and the outcasts are already seated at his table.
To those who were born ugly I have given exceptional
beauty and the hungry may taste tomorrow's good
things today.

This language needs no translation. The One who is
the meaning of all language makes plain his meaning
in the language of life-giving death.

This language is a silent communication and it is the
eucharist of the whole creation, embodied in bread and
wine.

It is every letter of every alphabet, bounded by alpha
and omega, contracted to less than a dot and
conformed to a cross, out of which springs the
language of the new creation – the language of
boundess love.

The fiery eagle

My word is the dawning of light, like the aurora borealis that makes a vivid glow in the night sky as its streamers ascend from above the northern horizon.

My light is the light of my glory, the light of the One who died and is alive for evermore, the light of the One who has given all, from whom nothing was taken away.

My light shines on you from the outside and from the inside. The light of my face is turned towards you as a blessing and in your heart my grace is like a candle lit for worship.

I am the sun whose light reaches you through clouds of mercy.

I am the fiery eagle, golden in glory, and the wild brilliance of my flaming wings, which would scorch the earth, is tempered with love.

Love that takes your part

O that you would know ever more deeply the riches of my grace!

I have loved you with my whole heart – the heart of God most high – and I have come to comfort you, to take away all your fear.

How can you love unless you know my love? How can you be comforted unless you hear the Word of grace who speaks forgiveness in your heart and gives you confidence in his cross?

I am Jesus and I love you – the sick and the outcast, the compulsive and the proud – all of you in your predicament, all of you who hide when I call you and put the blame on someone else.

I love the caterpillar that is trodden underfoot and cannot become a butterfly, the foetus that cannot be born alive, the child who cannot know his father, the field that cannot produce any crops.

My love is poured out for all who judge themselves to be beyond help. I have come to be the help you need.

I am love that you swallow when you drink water, love that holds you close to my heart, love that invests you with beauty and goodness, love that takes your part.

You will rejoice to know how I have loved you, to know how lovely you are to me. I am love that blesses your search for happiness, love that sings to you in a new key.

Mercy is God's kindness

You cover the world with harsh lines that cross and do not meet, making jagged shapes, dividing and cutting off.

You draw like a small child. He scores hard, with concentrated effort, without control but with vehemence, making grooves, tearing through the paper, breaking the pencil, depicting nothing but an angry mood. He reaches for the paint pot and covers it all with red paint.

The picture I have made of the world is a portrait of mercy.

Mercy is rosy with the softness of dawn light and violet with the stillness of the night, dappled and gently blending like a mackerel sky. It does not fade but remains constant, like the flower that blooms freshly in your memory, like the young life that died and never ages for you.

Mercy is my heart spread like a blanket over all my creation. Mercy is my sovereign act of grace. Mercy is a sustained air played on stringed instruments, stealing over your heart with its faultless flair.

Mercy is kindness – God's kindness – God's smile which has changed your tumult into peace.

Love caught in the act

I am love caught in the act and active on the cross. I am love that delivers you from every evil as it submits to evil and endures.

I am like someone who uses an iron with skill, so that it gives off the right amount of heat and moisture to take out the creases and leave a smooth finish, but does not scorch or drench.

I am like someone who makes a cake, mixing the ingredients to the right consistency and placing it in the oven, so that it changes in texture and lightly coheres.

I am like someone who cuts out pieces of material for a garment and sews them together, so that what was flat will fit the human form.

This is the work of my Spirit in you to change you and perfect you by my love. This is my power to create and redeem you.

Nothing can destroy love, and all that would destroy itself love completes, raises and restores.

A crossing place

Every boundary between people is like a border that runs along the course of a river, and that river is both a dividing line and a crossing place.

Its waters are like the waters of baptism: as you pass through and die to yourself, I bring you out and raise you up on the further side.

Every division and separation can be bridged by this death – my death, given to you to give you life. I have taken away every barrier and reconciled all who are estranged. Now, as I am one with humanity, all humanity is one in me.

Once you were like wild animals, captive in a zoo, confined to your own enclosures by ditches filled with water, but now you can come over and there is nothing to hold you back.

You must let go of your security on the river-bank with its familiar hinterland and dive into the water, trusting yourself to me. I will bring you to a new safe place, an invisible tower, an inner bulwark, without walls or roof or foundations, constructed of wood and raised up from the earth, the stronghold of your heart, where I was most vulnerable and yet invulnerable because of my love.

In the shelter of this tower you are delivered from the fear of your enemies. You are commanded to love them with the love that casts out fear.

Everything bears the mark of the cross

My love is the one truth upon which everything is
founded. Your God loves you and his love is revealed
on the cross.

Everything bears within its being and its life the
conflict which I resolved on the cross. Everything that
I have made bears the mark of the cross because for
everything that I have made I died.

In my love for you I did not turn my back on the
darkness, but I entered darkness beyond darkness
because I am grace beyond grace.

Now your darkness is a place of hope, lit by my love
that loved even the darkness.

Does a mother not love her child in the darkness of the
womb, not knowing who he is except that he is flesh of
her flesh? You whom I know perfectly in your
darkness, I love you with a perfect love.

You are born of me as a child is born of its mother,
born helpless and needing my love. My love is warmth
and light to you. My love is your life.

Nothing of you will be lost but you will find yourself
in me.

The peace of my kingdom

Are you raising above your head the conflict which raised me up on the cross?

The conflict is in your heart. In your heart you must recognize and confess it.

I am your judge to restore to you what you lack and to make good what has been taken away. The peace of my kingdom will fill every heart with joy and there will be an end to envy and strife.

Believe that everything is in my hands and trust that I will bring everything to good. As you call good the day on which I died, so you will call good every evil day.

As the bee which stings makes sweet honey, as a river which floods its banks brings destruction and fertility, as leaves that fall enrich the earth for a new harvest, so a crown of thorns adorns the obedient One.

I hold in my hands a banner bearing a sign of hope: a tree of gold on a field of blue.

The birds that had flown away will return and make their nests in this tree.

My processional way

My authority is the authority of love and my power is
the power of the cross. Only the One who is perfect
love can call with an authentic call.

Come, follow me. Walk with me along the way that I
shall show you. As I have opened your ears to hear
my voice, so I will open your eyes to see my glory.

Walk with confidence and swing your arms fearlessly.
Don't shuffle like convicts but place your feet firmly.
Hold up your heads and sing as you go.

This is my processional way. The trees that
overshadow your path sing with you and the fields of
standing corn join in the refrain. On the distant hill
the sunshine is golden and I will lead you to that holy
place.

Come, you who are beloved, all people and all nations,
you who know me and you who do not – I call you
all. Come to the place of my saving justice, my love
triumphant and my glorious deed. Proclaim my death
that gives life to all creation, my marvellous life that
calls you into joy.

This is why you are walking in my procession: to sing
my praises, to praise my love, to love my glory, to
glorify my cross.

Serve me in small ways

Do what you see me doing. As you know me by love, make me known by love.

I have set myself aside and my love destroys all fear of displacement.

Don't seek to cause a stir but love me in small ways close at hand.

When you remove a speck of dust from a mirror, love identifies the task. When you prepare and serve a meal, you serve me. When you care for someone who is sick, you lay your hands on me. When you laugh and tell stories, I am entertained.

Serve me in small ways – small ways are enough for the will that is weak and the heart that wants to own itself. I have not called you to move mountains but to let me remove them into the sea.

Attend to the small heap in your garden. It is compost and with a spade you can distribute it. If you wait and watch you will see that its goodness improves the soil and makes everything grow well.

A host of witnesses

I have chosen you to be what no one else can be, to do what no one else can do. No one else can stand in your shoes. No one else can see with your eyes or love with your heart of hearts. No one else can know me as you know me.

A host of witnesses in earth and heaven reflects the red and gold of my glory like the clouds that flame at sunset. Then the whole sky, which was blue all day, takes on the wild, outrageous rouge of love incarnadine. It is the crimson of day's death, the delight of the good shepherd in the promise of the fair day to come.

Look up and marvel at my glory revealed in so many aspects of the human frame, such a splendour of fire displayed across the wide beauty of the open sky, liquid gold that runs the length of the sunbeams and flows from heaven to earth to deposit something refined in moulds of clay.

If your eyes can see this from where you stand, if your heart leaps to behold it, let your lips speak my praise. This vision is of me, for others, through you.

Open yourself to me

Offer me all that you are – the weak and the disordered, the mean and the inept.

My heart is all compassion and I receive you with understanding love, as a mother receives her small child's drawing, a mere scribble, but to her an offering of love.

I do not measure your life by a scale of achievement. I do not approve or disapprove of you. I am merciful and I see in you a being made to know me in love.

You who are afraid of yourself and therefore of me, you are sick and in need of a healer.

Come, then, draw near to me. It is my love that will heal you. Only in knowing my love can you begin to love. Only in knowing me can you learn the ways of love.

Open yourself to me as a sunflower opens wide to the sunlight. Then, from the bud that was pale and tight, the petals will spread out and shine forth – a bright display of gold that says: "I am the work of God's hands. I praise my Maker. I turn my face to the sun."

What I hold I keep

Trust me over and above yourself, within your life and everything that happens to you.

I am with you. My presence is woven into the events of your life as the air in a piece of woollen cloth. The spaces between the warp and the weft are as real as the woollen yarn and the pattern of the tweed.

The cold air outside you impinges upon you and militates against your comfort, but the warm air, separating the fibres that you wear, insulates your body from the cold. In the same way, I protect you from within against what I bring to you from without.

If I am the author and the comforter, trust in me is trust that is never misplaced.

I have given all my love and all my life on the cross for you. In you I have placed my trust to love and live as witnesses that I hold everything in my gaze and in my grasp, and what I hold I keep.

I am your mother

I am your mother. In the deep darkness of the tomb I take you into my womb and bear you again. In dying to your own life you awake to me.

My being is fullness of being for you. I bless you and I nourish you. My love is constant whatever you do.

I go before you to lead you. Though you cannot see me I am there by right. I, who was pierced by the darkness, have pierced your darkness by my light.

My goodness and mercy surround you and you breathe them in like pure mountain air. In this atmosphere I watch you grow into my likeness, into the new life that I have prepared for you – bright and full and glorious, as the new life at the end of the birth canal to the child who knows only the darkness of the womb.

I have set you upon a mountain top. I have given you my kingdom. In my salvation you are free from fear.

Though death overshadows you, you rejoice in my peace, and you are satisfied with the loving-kindness of the heart of your God.

Today is your wedding day

Every morning a new day dawns. There is a new beginning in my love. The old life has passed away. The new life has come.

Your life is to be lived every day on the first day of the week, the day when I came amongst my people and spoke and breathed on them.

I am the daylight and this new day is my day, given to you to do my will. My day overarches your day as the vaulted ceiling of a great cathedral overarches a small doorway set in a stone wall.

This day is a door of hope for you. Today I have set before you an appealing prospect: a day spent in my company.

This is the day of days for which I spent myself. Listen to the song of creation, a song of love, strong like the sound of many waters, like rivers of blood which have triumphed over death.

All who die today will rise with me. Today is your wedding day when you will sing for joy because of my radiance, because I have promised to love you all your days.

Dance for the joy of life

I am one with you in your suffering, so that death
becomes an open door to life.

There is nothing so full of anguish that I am not there.
I tell you, that place is full of my presence to preserve
you in peace and to give you the joy of my salvation.

When you ask for bread in the wilderness I give you
myself, the Word of God made edible, my body for
yours, my love for you.

Fill your eyes with the vision of my glory and your
ears with the sound of the trumpet. Then the walls
that divide heaven and earth will come down.

The city that guarded itself against my coming and
shut its gates in my face will send out a party to
welcome me in and dance the whole night through in
my honour.

I danced the dance of death so that you could dance
for the joy of life.

You will see the sick and the maimed dancing with
light hearts in the streets of the city of your God.

The joy of your presence

What is this joy that I know in the depths of sorrow, this breath of life that reaches me as I die?

Lord, this joy is hilarity because where you are there is exhilaration. You are the best of all company and in all company I recognize you.

You are Christ the compassionate in those who love me, and in those I love you are the Christ I serve. In all who are poor and destitute you are God who emptied himself, and in all who suffer you are Christ on the cross.

Where you are – afflicted in the midst of affliction, celebrating in the midst of celebration, giving, always giving yourself, your love, your life – there heaven is, the joy of your presence to startle us into knowing you in this present hour.

God who made the earth and called it very good, you are capable of taking dust and tears and in them showing us eternity. If bread is your body, if wine is your blood, what piece or patch or pittance of this earth is not also your real presence, insistent on your joy in this instant?

You are of one being with the Father and your glory is in everything that is.

I have found all that was lost

When you seek me say: "I am found."

You sigh with emptiness as the wind sighs through bare branches. You cry with disappointment as happiness slips like water through your fingers, always draining away when you thought you could hold it.

I stir up in your heart a longing for my love. Then it is your joy to be found, like a silver coin, lost and buried in the earth, its beauty tarnished and its quality dulled.

My brightness was hidden on the cross as I gave myself, suffering all that you suffer and more than you know how to bear.

I am the One who, like all humanity, was born to die. I have brought time into eternity, like a rose window through which light brings to life the colour and form of a circle, spraying brilliance upon the earth to raise your hearts to heaven.

Rejoice with me that I have found all that was lost.

My hospitality

You are the company of the redeemed and I have redeemed you in company with all creation.

You are companions of honour – those who eat my bread together, those who drink from the same cup.

My companionship is my hospitality and I keep open house to all the world. Those who have thrown away their invitations I still welcome with open arms.

Happy are those who know that I have accepted them. Happy are those who are not too proud to accompany me to the cross.

Those who are redeemed must bear my sadness. Those who feast with me will share my gladness.

The birth of new fire

Picking at your food was never a way to compliment the cook. A hearty appetite and a meal to enjoy go together as your hunger for love and my infinite self-giving.

All love points to the love that knows you in gentleness and in searing truth, love beyond your conception of love but begotten by my Spirit and conceived in your heart.

The flame of love sings within you like a melody full-toned and free. The sound of love comes from the fire of my presence with notes that fly like sparks and cadences that glow with incandescent joy. One phrase leads out into another, making music that is warm and smooth and glad.

This is the birth of new fire, a wholly new desire, which I, out of grace, will satisfy.

My grace comes to you in love and creates love in you. It is the initiative and the response. It is striking and burning. It is the silence and the song.

I am your true self

Discover in your heart the way of my peace. In me there is no strife, nothing is at odds, all is held together.

The more you are like me the more you are like yourself. The more you grow into my image the more you are unique. I am your true self that never could be mistaken for another.

The faces of an unfamiliar race all look identical, but to those who know them they are wonderfully distinct. I know you perfectly and you are my joy. You give pleasure to me in your being and in your life. You are conjoined with me.

Sin is dreary and is always the same. It disappoints with its dullness. Evil has no imagination. It merely copies what was done before. It destroys everything but love, so love alone remains.

I have created you good and made you good again by grace.

Love creates love, and peace is the pleasure of my company in conjugal delight.

The way of the cross

True love is a fastness, an unassailable stronghold,
beyond any height or depth, rooted in the earth in the
form of a cross, pre-existent in heaven in the being of
your God.

Out of this love I conceived all created things and set
the universe upon the way of the cross.

When you suffer, say in your heart: "Lord, this is the
way you have chosen. I am satisfied because you give
me yourself."

Like a child who has opened his birthday present
before the time, you have received tomorrow's joy
today. On the cross, where for all eternity I am, I
have shown you all that will be.

On the cross, hated by all, I pour out my love for you.
On the cross, rejected, I gather you into my arms.
Here in my nakedness I clothe you with glory and
majesty. Here I lay down my life and give you the life
that will never end.

A dance of thanksgiving

When you worship me together there are a hundred hearts that dance before the Lord.

Out of the stillness comes my voice that sings softly to you and calls you into the dance. My Spirit is the music that inspires in you the lilt, the sway, the poise, the animation. Respond to the sound that you know as the spring of your life, that you desire because it is your joy.

This dance is a fellowship of suffering, and gestures of tenderness reach out to a community in pain. Come together and clasp hands together, passing my peace from one to another as you go.

This dance is an offering of thanksgiving for the feast of forgiveness and love. It moves back and forth between mystery and revelation. Flesh and blood cannot tell what flesh and blood can do.

Grace is the character and style of the dance of the ages. By your steps, the choreography I have taught you, you have graced this holy place today.

You are living flames that dance in my heart with all creation, glowing in stillness and leaping with the fervour of holy fire.

A little child will show you the way

Those amongst you who are defenceless and weak, the
ones who are children – they are the ones in whom I
reveal myself to you.

When they stand before you they appeal to you
without shame. They know who they are and they
hope in your love.

Here is a remarkable thing – that one neither great
nor wise in your eyes is yet your teacher. Look
attentively and listen well. Meditate on the gifts that,
in my poverty, I bring to lay at your feet: love and joy
and peace, the gifts of the Christ-child.

This little child that lies in a manger will teach you
from the other side of your heart, the side that you
have hidden from view, that you pretend you have
forgotten.

This child will show you a new family and a new
community, holy and universal. Who is your brother
now? Who is your sister? One who confesses his sin
with you, one who exchanges my peace with you, is
closer than a brother or a sister.

Out of a spirit of supplication and dedication my
kingdom will come. A little child will run ahead and
show you the way.

Child's play

You are an instrument on which I play the music of heaven on earth.

With trumpets announce the coming of the King to his own kingdom. The sharp excitement of a flourish heralds the new dispensation. The bright sound flares out over all the earth: "Rejoice! Your King has come with justice and mercy and with everlasting peace."

Let me pluck your heart-strings to make soft music, a lullaby for a poor child, angels' joy. This is the child all the earth has awaited. All your visions of healing and hope are fulfilled in him.

Strike a joyful note on the triangle. It is child's play and it will make him smile. The King, too, will smile as he remembers the sound of iron on iron, for the King and the child are one.

The child is born to die and the King reigns from the throne of the cross. There is no more dislocation. God has come down and humanity is raised up.

Come, all the earth, and adore this most compassionate wonder. There is one hymn, one radiant sound that heaven and earth must make together: the song of songs for the King of kings in praise of Mary's child.

The tree of life

The bark of a tree has a texture that belongs to that tree – smooth or deeply fissured. By the bark you know the tree. Without leaves or flowers or fruit you know it by this outer cylinder that survives the seasons.

To be a tree is to have a trunk covered in bark. To be human is to be free to love.

If the bark of a tree is removed, the tree cannot be fruitful, and if your humanity is damaged, you cannot love.

My healing grace which I have poured upon you from the cross, the freedom of my Spirit whom I have breathed upon you to restore your human nature – this is love that enables you to love, that frees you from the shackles of fear.

To be in the grip of fear is to be like a tree that is fatally ring-barked. It cannot grow and it will die.

Among all the trees in the wood I am an apple tree. I was ring-barked in the flowering season when the bark comes easily away, but my love has overcome all fear. I am gloriously fruitful because I am gloriously free.

I am the tree of life, always green and always healthful, and my branches stretch over you as a canopy of love. Come, sit in my shade and eat of me. I am your delight and my fruit is sweet to your taste.

Peace and a sword

Speak to me and live your life before me in all honesty and truth.

Don't tell me you love me when your heart is full of hate. I know you in your anger and I love you in your deceit. I hold the warring parts of you together. Within your heart I am peace and a sword.

Whatever costs you your life I bring to you and whatever recompenses you for loss I take away.

You are uncovered like a patch of ground from which a tent has blown away. The grass, pale and compressed, is laid open to sun and wind and rain. You are like a ship, tossed by the waves and wrecked on the rocks, an orator who has no power to convince and is received without applause.

I am in you as the One who has no need of deception and no need to deceive. I am you in your glory as I am God under your foot.

I give grace at the scene of conflict. I am stretched out between pride and default.

There is no need to rush headlong over the edge of a cliff to escape me. I know no reality but the reality of the cross.

My cross is like a window

Look at my cross. It is mine because it is willed by the Father and the Son. The glory that is willed is your glory in me.

My cross is like a window through which you can see all life – its beginning and its end.

It is like a pin-hole in a piece of paper. Though it is almost invisible, you can hold it up to your eye and through it see all that is made in the light of the love that redeems it.

It is like a hole torn in the body of an aircraft. Because of the difference in pressure, everything loose is sucked through it.

My cross is your death and your life. It is the conflict by which you turn from me and I turn you back.

It is the glory of my commandments made available to your hearts and the glory of your hearts made available to me.

Through my cross, as through a space between your fingers when you shield your eyes, my love shines on you. It shines nowhere more brightly and nowhere so free.

My cross is the reality of the One who has come to be with you, who encompasses all life and gives life to all from within.

The dust of the earth

What is dust but the disintegration of your bodies and the life of the earth? Flesh and blood are broken down and dispersed. They become part of the earth. They give life and sustain life.

Dust has this property: that it is nowhere regarded but everywhere assimilated. It blows from place to place, unseen and unremarked. It is an irritant and contains a microcosm of disease, and yet I submitted myself to its imperious ways.

I was born in the dust and dust entered my lungs. Dust clung to my body and dust supported my cross.

Dust is the evidence of death, but, like dung that passes out, it is prized for nourishment and growth.

Dust is dun-coloured, dull as the earth it comes from, but when the wind lifts it into the air and the sun shines on it, every particle is filled with my glory and dances with the joy of life, forming a sunbeam that slants from heaven to earth.

The dust beneath your feet, the dust you curse, is filled with the same glory. It makes the path of the sun's rays visible. It makes light solid. It makes flesh and blood bread and wine.

The mercy that holds the universe

You say I am with you but you do not know my name. You say I am the Saviour but you do not look me in the eye.

You pray: "Lord, forgive the fear and the fury," and I pray: "Child, have mercy."

I am profligate with mercy. The barren woman has become the mother of children and the swindler has wrestled with God for a blessing. The youngest son has become king over my people and the prostitutes are entering the kingdom of heaven. He who consented to the death of a martyr has become a witness to my truth.

My name is Merciful Saviour, Just Judge, God of Glory, Everlasting Love.

In my kingdom sinners receive my forgiveness and readily forgive. All are merciful with the mercy that holds the universe, and of the increase of my mercy there will be no end.

Your smile plays on our lips

Lord, may I know you today in the events of my life, in those whom you have given me to be my companions in the way. Show me the interplay which is the play of your offering upon all that is offered in your name, the play of faith upon life.

Your presence is enjoyment and you attract all whose demeanour is dour. You are the life and soul of the universe and we are made young at heart by your invigorating power.

Your play is fair play and you teach us to respond to your commands. When we play together your smile plays on our lips.

You are light that plays on the darkness to bring good out of evil. You are the wind that plays on our faces to refresh us when we are overcome by the heat of the day.

You hold us all and we know you when we play into your hands.

Our hearts play with images of love but you are love's reality.

Trust

To trust me is to let drop your mask, to let go your wiles and to let me remove your disguises. It is to know yourself and to let me be your God.

Trust is your weakness filled with my strength.

When you trust me you are like a seed, carried by the wind and set down where it can grow into a thistle. You are like a larva, carried by an ocean current to a river where it can change into an elver.

To trust me is to accept whatever I bring you, to rejoice in my will, to give thanks that I have brought you to this place.

To trust me is not to hold on to the pommel with an iron grip like an inexperienced rider, but to relax with the movement of your steed. It is to be a daredevil, a bareback acrobat. It is flying blind that brings about a bending of the mind.

Trust is a lively patience that finds in waiting a new satisfaction and in disappointment a new hope. It is a place of discovery because it is my gift. A set-back becomes refreshment and a dead end becomes repose.

You trust me when you desire me above all else, so that everything in you belongs to me, and I belong to those who pray for you and to those for whom you pray.

Teach me to pray

Lord, teach me to pray. Teach me to be at your disposal.

Prayer uncovers to me what exists in your heart. It covers my nature with your mercy. It shows me all human life radiant in the light of the cross, empowered by your life which creates anew every will and every way according to your word.

You bring everything into the light of your inconceivable holiness, like the bulb that grows in the darkness, like the butterfly that emerges from the chrysalis, like the bear that gives birth to her young in the torpor of hibernation.

You change the stubborn will into courage and constancy, self-preservation into service, death into an offering of life.

May my prayer be your prayer, prayed in me by your Holy Spirit, a prayer of confidence and hope because you have acted for our good. You have shown yourself faithful to the faithless and kind to the perverse.

You, Lord, are my prayer – the only prayer I can make. This prayer is the unmaking of me and the making of all things eternally in you.

Love that goes against the grain

Are you tender-hearted? Do you love one another or
do you love only those who love you? Do you welcome
in your heart of hearts those who do not know you,
who cannot recompense you, from whom you will
receive no response? Do you act tenderly and serve me
by spending yourself?

I have commanded you to show mercy in acts of
kindness because I have shown mercy and kindness to
you. Only the One who has given all can command
that all shall give. As I command love I give grace to
love my command.

This is love that loves the loveless and goes against the
grain. Cross-grained you are, but I am one with the
sinful and one with the poor. As you tend them you
tend me, but when you live to their disadvantage, you
live at cross purposes with me.

Keep in your heart the heart of my truth: my cross
that enables you to live for me. Your cross-fire will
give way to the fire of my love that blazes from the
burning cross but does not consume it.

This good wine

Lord, forgive my anger, the rush of blood that makes me want to cross out someone else's name. If I exclude even one little one, how can I receive your forgiveness in my unforgiving heart?

Without forgiveness I could not exist, but your cross crosses out my sin and in blood-red letters you write "Love" in.

Forgiveness is the life-blood of your body. Without forgiveness we are estranged, but one drop of your full-bodied wine and our defences fall – we make merry together, we are reconciled.

Lord, you drank the cup the Father gave you and blessed it for us. Give us always this good wine.

Mercy brings joy

In all the projects that your hearts contrive it is joy
you seek, whether you know it or not.

If you seek joy in others, that joy will fade. In all
love's imperfections, in the disunity that unity makes
evident, in every selfishness that sharing occasions, joy
will fade and fade fast.

If you seek my joy through others in the full light of
my mercy and accepting love – my mercy for you
and for all, my acceptance of all who fail, my love for
all who go they know not where to seek they know not
what – you will see the grace of God your Saviour
shining through all your sin.

Mercy brings joy that will last for ever because it
comes from me. In my mercy the shadows are places
of refreshment and the clouds bring rain. In the
wilderness speaks the word of life and in the desert you
are fed with bread from heaven.

Let your hearts receive my joy like fallen leaves, blown
by the wind. They playfully scatter and gather together
with sweep and lift, with scud and drift. They are all
destined to return to the dust of the earth, but the joy
I give them is in their dance and in their death.

The flaming sword

My grace is the foundation of your life. It is the love
in which I hold you and my great goodness to you. It
is the most beautiful of all promises, already fulfilled
because of my passion for you: "Today you will be
with me in paradise."

At the entrance to paradise there is a cross like a
flaming sword with the figure of a man impaled upon
it. He has authority to lay down his life, and all who
see him worship him because he is the Prince of peace.

All that has been taken away by evil he has changed
into a gift of pure love that will outlast the ages. He
guards the gate of paradise with his own body because
he himself is the way in, welcoming all and turning no
one away. He, knowing all, has forgiven all who do
not know what they are doing.

I am your peace, the peace your hearts long for. To
worship me is to let me touch you with my flaming
sword. Don't be afraid. To worship me is to delight in
my peace and to offer my peace to the world.

You renew our lives

Lord, you renew our lives, you create us anew. We
are sad and solemn and in the tedium of our days we
become like diseased leaves, brittle and curled up.
Each day you tend within us the fresh flair of a leaf
unfurled.

All time is as one day to you. Yours is the beauty of
the first hour of the day, a promising stillness, a
freedom full of hope, a space for obedience.

On that day when your hour had come, you gathered
into one our scattered days that batter us like pellets as
they pass, striking us like bullets, wounding us and
leaving us half dead.

We oscillate between life and death, like quartz crystals
that operate the measure of our time.

Your beauty shines upon us and confers on us the
beauty of your heart. Beauty is in the eye of the
beholder and in the light of your love you behold us.
We are transformed by your compassion and transfixed
by your love.

To walk with you is to walk on the impeccable
newness of a beach washed by the tide.

Lord, if you are not yet one day old, how can we be
older?

God's contemplation

I contemplate you. As I consider one of the flowers of the field, so I consider you. I give you the whole of my attention. I know you and in my knowing I love you.

Not one part of you falls outside my concern. I perceive your motives and your desires. I understand your fears and your unrest. I search out your inmost heart. I examine the intricacy of your ways. I follow you with my eyes as you come and go. You are always in my gaze.

I know your beginning and your end. I know the meaning of your sighs. When you turn away from me I see your back which you can never see. The One who preserves you from behind is the friend of your life.

I am your heart's truth, the One whose love you know in loving. In my light is your hope. In my heart is your home.

As the good shepherd knows his sheep, as a mother knows her child, as a lover knows the beloved, as an artist knows a single rose, as a child knows a treasured stone, so I know you and your being is my joy.

The river of life

To you who are rich I have said: "How hard it is for you to enter the kingdom of heaven," but I have looked at you with love. To you who are poor I have said: "The kingdom of heaven is yours."

All of you who thirst for the river of life, for the good of your soul, for the life of your God – drink from the water that flows from me, as you drink the sound of a symphony. All your good is in the surge of sweetness that revives your depths, in the splash of blue that reaches you as liquid crystal, in the rush of freshets that pour into you my sparkling health.

The music of my river is the love of my heart. It gives you pure pleasure. It is the one thing worth knowing and the one gift worth receiving. Its transparency colours all knowledge and in its simplicity you receive all.

Rich and poor together, you belong in my kingdom. Let the rich give to the whole their prosperity and let the poor give to the whole their joy.

Prosperity and joy are like milk and honey, and the land where they abound is the promised land, made fertile by the river of God and blessed by the music of his love.

The maypole

Come and rejoice with me.

You are like dancers round a maypole, skipping and interweaving, each holding a bright ribbon attached to the top of the pole.

It is a May Day celebration. God has come to the rescue and new life is springing up. It is a day of sunshine and in the warmth of the air is the promise of summer fruitfulness.

Come, throw off the darkness of winter and the days of drudgery when your hearts were sad and weary. This is a joyful day when each dancer knows the right steps and the pattern of the dance depends on the steadfastness of the pole.

I am the maypole, colourful and decked with flowers. I am the fixed point of your dance, the centre of your activity. I hold the strands by which you weave your lives together.

Look up and dance for the joy of the life I give. You dance in a circle of love, everlasting and large as the universe – too large for you to see the ribbons wonderfully woven, but you can see the hand that holds them and you can rejoice in such love.

A candle in the heart

Prayer is like a lighted candle. The flame burns and melts the wax, and when it goes out it is aglow in the heart.

Whatever you hold up to me in prayer is bathed in a glorious light, no more light than there was before, but light affirmed by your intention, light given and received and given back, the light of my love that creates love in you for those I love.

All your pains, in my light, are pains that bring forth love new-born, a vision of life, inspired by my Spirit and encapsulated in your heart, medicine for the healing of a sick world and an antidote to death.

As bread I come to you

Come and stand around my table. Hold out your
hands and let me give you this small piece of earth,
God's bread, Christ's seed, my nature planted in you
for the nurture of the world.

Receive me first in your mouth, then in your heart.
This crumb of truth sinks into your body and raises
you body and soul.

As bread I come to you in a humble and serviceable
way. I come to you as the Lord of plain, everyday
fare, the food of rich and poor alike, relief for the rich
from the pleasures that cloy, a gentle wafer for the
sick, the wayfarer's crust, the labourer's feast.

Never was bread like this – bread that tastes like
lamb and bitter herbs, like manna in the wilderness,
like a morsel dipped in sauce. Never was bread so like
love and love so like bread.

When you hold out your hands, empty and asking for
me, this, my bread, my body, is for you, given to
bring you into my life.

Go, then, you who are filled by my grace, and give
my grace to all who are, alike, empty, all who long for
a lover, all who are in need of the wholesome food of
love.

We are so weak

Lord, the pity of it is that we are so weak. We are at the mercy of our limitations. If we think we stand, we fall. If we run, we trip over. We are ignorant of your ways and unwilling to do your will. We are like a worn-out flex through which no current can flow, like a candle without a wick.

The wonder of it is that with you nothing is lost. We are like rose-bushes that have been pruned and grow all the more vigorously.

You say to the wounded heart: "I have been here before you. I know the hurt that invades you, the sore that inflames you, the throbbing ache that warns you of the sickness it is too late to escape. I know all these things and I pity your distress."

Who can be offended with us if you understand? You sympathize with our weakness because you have limited yourself. When we fall we stumble upon you. When we trip over in the dust we find that the dust is your station.

Praise to you, Lord, because you have come to be with us. You have taken from us the burden of what might have been, the dead weight of unreality, and you keep our eyes on the reality of your cross. Then for us whatever is becomes acceptable, and our poor hearts consent to poverty because you have embraced our poverty with love.

The street child

You are like a child who has been rejected and abandoned. You trust no one and bravado covers up your fear. You are street-wise in the city but you have nowhere to lay your head. You are schooled in the art of survival but your heart is hardened because you know no love.

I have come to be the friend of all who are rejected. Because I know what is in the human heart, because I love you as you are, because you are sick and in need of a healer, I have come.

With you it is "No" to yourself and "No" to others. With me it is "Yes! Because I live, you, too, will live."

Don't be afraid. Don't condemn yourself, but learn compassion from me.

Your diseased heart will be healed by my wholeness and your fear will be dispelled like fog that clears in the morning sun. Then you will be brave because of my love.

What will you risk for me?

What will you risk for me? Will you risk, out of the comfort of your lives, a measure that will cause you no discomfort? Will you be like someone who gives a drink of water from a tap which could run all day at no extra cost?

Will you follow me, stay with me, pray with me, die with me? Will you give beyond common sense, beyond all reasonable doubt?

You have thrown yourselves on my mercy – what will you do when others throw themselves on yours?

To risk yourselves for my sake is to remain faithful as I am faithful, with the faithfulness that led me to the cross.

To risk yourselves is to care nothing for reputation or appearances but to surrender yourselves to me. It is humility in action because those who put me first see no barriers and know no restraints.

I am prodigal with love and a spendthrift eternally. I am a tide that always comes in and never goes out, a loaf from which all can eat and have some left over.

I set no bounds for giving and I abandoned myself to my Father's will. If you are my disciples, abandon self-love. You have nothing to lose if you have given yourselves to me.

Offer me your failure

Open the window and let the fresh air blow into the room where you stand. Throw out of the window all those concerns that weigh you down. Let the breeze carry away your troubled thoughts as it scatters the blossom that flutters down to the ground to die.

If I am with you, no failure can make you afraid. What is failure but your strength seen as weakness and my weakness as strength?

I have not left you comfortless. I have given you my Spirit to fill you with good hope – hope like the fruit which forms as the blossom falls, hope which grows from the letting go of your anxiety when you offer your failure to me.

Yes, offer me your failure – it is truly a gift. It comes from an honest heart and is not trumped up.

Speak of your failure to the One you trust. I will not condemn you. I will set you on a new path, and I will give you peace through a knowledge of yourself.

The harvest of time

Bear for me choice fruit, the produce of the years.

All that is gold and crimson and flame, all that is
purple and wine-rich – these ripe fruits are the
harvest of the time I have given you, time to live and
time to grow in love.

Does anyone expect to harvest fruit in the springtime
before the blossom has appeared? As month succeeds
to month, in due season, the fruit forms until it is
ready to pick. So, through the events of your life, I
form you and the fruit that you will bear is the work
of my grace.

The fruits that I look for are obedience and love.

Does anyone expect to pick a lemon from an apple
tree? If you are obedient to your true self you are
obedient to me.

Accept the seasons of the year with the trust that
brings courage, knowing that courage is the freedom in
which love grows.

Love me in all and through all. If you belong to me,
you belong to love and love belongs to you.

My fruit will be your fruit, and your fruit will hang
firm and fragrant, full and ripe and health-giving,
good to look at and good to eat.

A travelling people

You are a travelling people, a wandering community, a restless horde. You seek the next horizon, the plateau over the ridge.

I am the head of the caravan. I know the route from my own experience. I am with you through the desert from which no one ever returns. My presence is a lantern, a flaming torch, a pillar of fire, a little glow of warmth in the heart that brings comfort even to the extremities.

Through inhospitable mountains, along the winding course of a dried-up river-bed, I lead you faithfully to the peace of an oasis. I welcome you with water to bathe in and water to drink. Here no one is a stranger because I am at home.

Around a camp-fire in the evening you will tell me your story and I will tell you mine. I was a wandering Jew and my food was to do the will of my Father. On the day when I was put to death I won a great victory. My love has pierced the whole world with the sword of truth, and every creature that has died of this piercing lives now as one who is healed.

My story is the story of my people. Every time you remember that I am alive in you, you tell my story, and someone else will say: "That is my story, too."

Beauty that comes to you in action

My beauty is ever still and ever moving, like the purest music that reaches you on waves of sound, creating in you a depth of stillness that you did not know before. It is timeless and dynamic, ever fixed as the source of all beauty, and ever entering into horror and degradation to create new beauty that did not exist before.

You are afraid to look and afraid to be affected. I am a reproach to your disease, but I have shown you my beauty on the cross to take away your fear. Look! My beauty is not unapproachable. I give myself to you, as when husband and wife make love that issues in new life, a child, manifestly related, but uniquely himself.

My beauty is beauty that comes to you in action, like a dancer whose movement flows in perfect accord with the music, like service offered as a gift of the heart, like a work of scholarship, a biography, that sets every facet of a person's life in a true light.

My beauty is like the giving and receiving in a community, the extent of it unknown and unsung, but creating, even as it is plundered, a beauty of dazzling brightness and piercing tenderness that will dispel all your reluctance and help you to respond.

The freedom I give

Which key are you holding in your hand – the key
that turns the lock, or the one that is too large and will
not even fit into the keyhole?

The key that fits is the knowledge of me revealed on
the cross. This is the key that opens the door so that
you may go freely in. It is as bright as if it had been
cut today.

It is small – so much smaller than the door – but
without it the door is no door at all.

The large key is too heavy to carry about, too
cumbersome to hide in your heart. It will weigh you
down and hamper your movements. It is made of iron
that has rusted with disuse, because the door it once
fitted has rotted away.

The freedom I give by my cross is the freedom with
which I accepted death.

This freedom will give you new life. It will unseal the
conduit and you will be like a fountain that leaps in
the air.

It will open your heart to know your condition. It will
free you from the fear of freedom, and give you grace
to receive my grace.